CAMPFIRE COOKBOOK

50 + Awesome Meals You Can Prepare While Being Close to Mother Nature!

(A Collection of the Best Outdoor Camping Recipes)

Neil Spell

Published by Alex Howard

© Neil Spell

All Rights Reserved

Camping Cookbook: 50 + Awesome Meals You Can Prepare While Being Close to Mother Nature! (A Collection of the Best Outdoor Camping Recipes)

ISBN 978-1-990169-44-1

All rights reserved. No part of this guide may be reproduced in any form without permission in writing from the publisher except in the case of brief quotations embodied in critical articles or reviews.

Legal & Disclaimer

The information contained in this book is not designed to replace or take the place of any form of medicine or professional medical advice. The information in this book has been provided for educational and entertainment purposes only.

The information contained in this book has been compiled from sources deemed reliable, and it is accurate to the best of the Author's knowledge; however, the Author cannot guarantee its accuracy and validity and cannot be held liable for any errors or omissions. Changes are periodically made to this book. You must consult your doctor or get professional medical advice before using any of the suggested remedies, techniques, or information in this book.

Table of contents

PART 1 1

CAMP FIRE RECIPES 2

Craft beer sauce chicken 2
Camping pasta 4
Fire roasted plum turkey sandwiches 6
Rocky mountain BBQ burgers 7
Lemongrass chicken skewers 9
Avocado pumpkin quinoa salad 11
Swiss chard scramble with garlic toast 13
Grilled portabello pull-apart rubens 15
Tortilla española 17
Samosa baked potatoes 19
Black-eyed pea sausage skillet supper 20
Hobo chicken puttanesca 23
Campfire vampire steak 25
Foraged mushroom tempeh kabobs 26
Colorado elk stroganoff 28
Colorado pesto mushroom sandwiches 30
Wild dandelion greens salad 32
Bacon campfire potato with wild onions 33
Cilantro lime olathe sweet corn 35
Dutch oven baked beans 36
Wild onion potato salad 38
Fireside feta with thyme 40
Colorado cantaloupe and prosciutto salad 42
Skillet mac and cheese crisp 43
Campfire jalapeño poppers 45
Garlic baby broccoli 46
Grilled palisade peach salad with goat cheese 47
3 bean salad 49
Heirloom carrot and apple slaw 51
Black-eyed pea summer salad 52

Goat cheese pasta salad with basil oil 53
Summer squash gremolata 54
Pimientos de padrón 55
Pear prosciutto and wild dandelion green bites... 56
Pickled slaw 57
Cucumber lime salad 58
Flame kissed watermelon salad 59
Cider vinegar baby spinach 61
Olathe sweet corn bread 62
Halloumi vegetable skewers 64
Quinoa with fresh herbs 65
Pie iron apple pie 68
Banana boats 70
Colorado s'mores 71
Dutch oven peach cobbler 72
Dulce de leche apricot kebobs 73
Salty peanut butter chocolate s'mores 74

CONCLUSION 75

PART 2 76

INTRODUCTION 77

C Lazy U "Woodsie" Trout Breakfast 78
Honey Sweet Potato Breakfast Burritos 81
Wild Strawberry Yogurt Parfait 83
Foraged Porcini Mushroom Egg Scramble 85
Smoked Colorado Foil Breakfast 87
Chewy Cherry Breakfast Rounds 89
Apple Butter Flapjacks 91
Wild Chokecherry Jelly And Biscuits 93
Pigs In A Morning Blanket 97
Denver Omelette 99
Pepper Bacon & Egg Breakfast Sandwiches 101
Maple Cream Cheese French Toast 103
Breakfast Bagels With Cilantro Sauce 105
Colorado Honey Almond Granola 107

Dutch Oven Honey Monkey Bread	109
Hearty Mountain Breakfast	111
Cardamom Spiced Oatmeal	113
Colorado Stout Pancakes	115
Green Chile Breakfast Burritos	117
Kale And Goat Cheese Cups	119
Apple Cinnamon Granola	121
Sweet Potato Pancakes	123
Brown Sugar Grilled Grapefruit	125
Cheesy Jalapeño Scrambled Eggs	126
Breakfast Quinoa Bowls	127
Green Chile Skillet Tots	131
Campfire Quesadillas	132
Hatch Green Chile Grilled Cheese	135
Hobo Packets With Foraged Wild Onions	137
Buffalo Chicken Tinfoil Baked Potatoes	139
Colorado Elk Sausage Campfire Pizza	141
Grammy's Corn Crusted Rainbow Trout	143
Bruschetta Baked Potatoes	145
Foraged Purslane Chickpea Tahini Wraps	146
Hipster Hobo Hash	149
Giant Pigs In A Blanket On A Stick	151
Colorado Blue Cheese Buffalo Burgers	153
Hot Dogs With Homemade Chow Chow	155
Wine Marinated Steaks With Naan	158
Vegetarian Paella	161
Jerk Chicken Campfire Kabobs	164
Rosemary Colorado Lamb Sloppy Joes	166
Vegetarian Campfire Nachos	168
Foraged Porcini Mushroom Sausage Dinner	170
Chilaquiles With Salsa Verde	173
Honey Chicken And Biscuit Sandwiches	176
Colorado Beer Brats	178
Elk Meatballs	180
Mustard Butternut Squash And Kale	182
Smoked Fingerling Potato Skillet Supper	184

GRILLED PESTO AND PEPPER SANDWICHES 186
PURPLE POTATO PIZZA 188
FOIL SWEET POTATOES WITH BLACK BEAN SALSA 190

Part 1

Camp fire recipes

Craft beer sauce chicken

Serves 4

Nothing tastes better while camping in Colorado than a local Colorado brew. I don't need to tell you that you have a few to choose from. This chicken, pairs perfectly with beer. I prefer an IPA in this recipe but you can use your favorite craft beer.

1 tablespoon olive oil

himalayan salt and freshly ground black pepper to taste

4 skinless, boneless chicken breasts

1 shallot, thinly sliced

½ cup Colorado craft beer

1 tablespoon soy sauce

2 tablespoons whole grain Dijon mustard

1 tablespoon Colorado honey

2 tablespoons fresh parsley, chopped

Heat the oil in a large cast iron skillet over hot coals or on a portable gas grill. Liberally sprinkle salt and pepper over the chicken breasts and add them to the pan.
Cook the chicken for 8 minutes on each side, or until well done. Remove from the pan and place on a plate. Cover to keep warm.
Add the shallot to the pan and sauté for 2 minutes. In a

small bowl whisk together the beer, soy sauce, mustard and honey. Add the beer mixture to the pan and bring to a boil. Stir a few times to loosen the cooked brown chicken bits on the bottom of the pan.
Cook until the sauce reduces, about 6 minutes. Return the chicken to the pan, spoon sauce over the chicken and cook for 3 minutes, or until heated through.
Sprinkle with fresh parsley and serve.

SUGGESTED BEVERAGE: Firestarter India Pale Ale – Bonfire Brewing Company (Eagle, Colorado)

Camping pasta
Serves 2

When you want a minimal amount of dishes, and a hearty vegetarian dinner, then look no further. Don't substitute the noodles for any whole wheat varieties. I love whole wheat pasta varieties, but they cook much slower, and will not work as well with this recipe.

2 tablespoons olive oil

1 yellow onion, chopped

4 cloves garlic, chopped

1 14.5 oz can crushed tomatoes

1 cup low sodium vegetable broth

dash red wine

1 cup fresh basil, chopped

1 tablespoon Italian seasoning

salt to taste

½ pound fusilli pasta noodles

½ cup Parmesan cheese

Heat the olive oil in a large fire safe pot over hot coals or on a portable gas stove. Add the onions and sauté for about 5 minutes. Add the garlic and cook for 1 minute more.

Add the tomatoes, with their juices, to the pot, along with the broth, red wine, a large pinch of the basil, Italian seasoning, salt and the pasta.

Cook covered, stirring often, to make sure the pasta is absorbing the liquid evenly. Cook for about 12 minutes, or until the pasta is al dente.

Remove from heat, spoon servings into bowls and top with the remaining fresh basil and Parmesan cheese.

SUGGESTED BEVERAGE: Sangre del Sol – Alfred Eames Cellars (Paonia, Colorado)

Fire roasted plum turkey sandwiches

Serves 2

Plums grow in many places in Colorado and when ripe, the juicy stone fruit goes great with summer basil and turkey. This hearty sandwich is a perfect camping dinner or you could enjoy for a hearty lunch.

3 garlic cloves, minced

3 tablespoons mayonnaise

freshly ground black pepper to taste

salt to taste

2 thick cut turkey cutlets

4 slices thick cut whole grain bread

1 Colorado plum, pitted and thinly sliced

10 basil leaves

At Home: Combine the garlic, mayonnaise and black pepper in a small jar or tupperware. Store in a cooler for camp.

At Camp: Sprinkle salt on the turkey cutlets and grill on a portable grill rack over hot coals in a campfire. Cook for about 5 minutes, flip, and cook for 5 minutes longer.

While the turkey cooks, place bread slices and plum slices on the grill and toast for 2 minutes on each side.

Remove the bread from the grill, spread the mayo mixture on 2 slices of bread then layer each slice with turkey, plums and basil leaves. Enclose the sandwich with the remaining slices of bread and serve warm.

SUGGESTED BEVERAGE: Colorado Red Ale – Black Shirt Brewing Company (Denver, Colorado)

Rocky mountain bbq burgers

Serves 4

Chock-full of grass-fed Colorado beef this burger is summer on a bun. I love barbecue sauce and it goes particularly well on these burgers.

1 tablespoon olive oil

1 yellow onion, thickly sliced

1 egg, lightly beaten

¼ cup quick cooking rolled oats

½ teaspoon garlic salt

½ teaspoon freshly ground black pepper

1 lb grass-fed Colorado beef

barbecue sauce

4 slices sharp cheddar cheese

4 hamburger buns

Heat the olive oil in a small skillet over hot coals in a campfire. Add the sliced onions and cook for about 10 minutes, or until caramelized.

Meanwhile, in a large bowl, combine the egg, rolled oats, garlic salt and pepper, stirring to combine. Add the beef and mix well. Using your hands, shape the beef mixture into 4 large hamburger patties.

Grill the hamburger patties on a portable grill rack over hot coals for about 8 minutes. Flip and grill for 8 minutes more, or until desired doneness.

Slather about a tablespoon of barbecue sauce on each burger within the last 5 minutes of cooking and top with a slice of cheddar cheese, allowing enough time for the cheese to melt.

Serve on hamburger buns with extra barbecue sauce and topped with the caramelized onions.

SUGGESTED BEVERAGE: Endpoint Triple IPA – Renegade Brewing Company (Denver, Colorado)

Lemongrass chicken skewers
Serves 2

It seems like I eat this dish every other camping trip during the summer. Served with a Colorado honey dipping sauce, the flavor is out of this world and a must try for your next outdoor adventure.

½ cup water

1 teaspoon sugar

2 ½ teaspoons Colorado wildflower honey

¼ teaspoon crushed red pepper

1 tablespoon white vinegar

1 tablespoon fish sauce

salt and freshly ground black pepper to taste

2 large stalks lemongrass, cut into 4 pieces each

¾ cup cilantro, chopped

½ cup olive oil

5 shallots, chopped

3 boneless skinless chicken breasts

½ cup mint leaves, torn

1 lime, cut into 4 wedges

At Home: In a small saucepan combine the water, sugar and honey. Simmer over medium heat, uncovered, for about 1 minute.
Pour the sauce into a bowl and add the red pepper. Let the sauce cool to room temperature and add the

vinegar, fish sauce, salt and black pepper. Stir to combine and store in a jar or tupperware in a cooler packed for camp.

Using a rolling pin, bruise the pieces of lemongrass and put them in a shallow dish that will fit in your cooler. Add the cilantro, olive oil and shallots to the dish and mix ingredients together. Cut the chicken breasts into 1 inch chunks and add to the dish, stirring to coat them well with the marinade. Cover and store for camp in a well iced cooler.

At Camp: Remove the chicken from the marinade and skewer the chunks on a green camping stick or skewers. Season the chicken with salt and pepper, then cook over the campfire, rotating slowly for about 10 minutes, or until the meat starts to slightly char and is cooked through.

Remove from the fire and let the chicken rest for 4 minutes before serving with the honey dipping sauce, mint leaves and lime wedges.

SUGGESTED BEVERAGE: Grasshop-ah – Colorado Cider Company (Denver, Colorado)

Avocado pumpkin quinoa salad
Serves 2

Fall in Colorado is filled with changing Aspen leaves, bugling elk and of course, pumpkins. This hearty salad can be eaten for lunch, but it also makes a great vegetarian dinner.

½ large pumpkin, peeled, seeded and cut into small chunks

1 teaspoon honey, plus 3 tablespoons for dressing

1 tablespoon balsamic vinegar

4 tablespoons olive oil

1 cup red quinoa, rinsed

1 ½ cups vegetable stock

3 tablespoons red wine vinegar

1 tablespoon whole grain mustard

1 lemon, juiced

freshly ground black pepper to taste

2 cups baby spinach

1 ripe avocado

1 pint cherry tomatoes

½ cup crumbled goat cheese

At Home: In tupperware combine the pumpkin chunks with 1 teaspoon honey, balsamic vinegar and 1 tablespoon of the olive oil. Store in a cooler for camp.

In a medium saucepan, combine the quinoa and vegetable stock and bring to a boil. Lower the heat to low and simmer, covered for about 15 minutes, or until the liquid has been absorbed. Remove from heat and let cool. Store in tupperware in a cooler for camp.

In a small jar combine the red wine vinegar, mustard, lemon juice, 3 tablespoons honey, 3 tablespoons of the olive oil and black pepper. Seal, shake and store in a cooler for camp.

At Camp: Place the pumpkin chunks on a large sheet of tinfoil. Fold edges around the pumpkin to seal and cook over hot coals for 15 minutes, or until they become tender.

Remove from heat and add the pumpkin, and pre-made red wine vinegar dressing to the quinoa, stirring to combine. Serve the pumpkin mixture over a bed of baby spinach and top with avocado, cherry tomatoes and crumbled goat cheese.

Serve while the pumpkin is still warm.

SUGGESTED BEVERAGE: Hey! Pumpkin Harvest Ale – Denver Beer Company (Denver, Colorado)

Swiss chard scramble with garlic toast

Serves 2

Of all vegetables, it seems swiss chard grows best in my Colorado garden. This healthy recipe utilizes fresh garden chard in a simple vegetarian dish accompanied by crunchy garlic toast.

2 tablespoons olive oil

1 small yellow onion, chopped

3 garlic cloves

¼ teaspoon crushed red pepper flakes

1 bunch swiss chard, about 6 large leaves, chopped

5 eggs

1 teaspoon turmeric

salt and freshly ground black pepper to taste

1 loaf bakery bread, sliced

Heat a large cast iron skillet over a campfire or portable gas stove. Add 1 tablespoon of the olive oil and swirl to coat the pan. Add the onion and cook for 5 minutes, or until tender.

Mince 2 garlic cloves and add them to the skillet along with the red pepper flakes. Cook for 1 minute longer. Add the swiss chard and cook for 5 minutes.

While the chard cooks, whisk the eggs in a large bowl with the turmeric and salt. Pour the eggs into the skillet and stir with the chard mixture until the eggs are cooked through, about 5 minutes.

While the eggs cook, toast bread slices over hot coals on a portable grill rack or on a green stick for about 3 minutes on each side of the bread slices. Cut the remaining garlic clove in half and rub the cut side of the garlic on the top side of the toast. Drizzle the remaining olive oil over the top of the bread and sprinkle with salt.

Remove the chard scramble from heat, sprinkle with black pepper and serve warm with the garlic toasts.

SUGGESTED BEVERAGE: Jean-Claude Van Blond – Wit's End Brewing Company (Denver, Colorado)

Grilled portabello pull-apart rubens
Serves 4

This delicious vegetarian sandwich features portabello mushrooms. If you prefer meat, simply swap the portabello for sliced corned beef. Baked in tinfoil in campfire coals this is one of my favorite camping treats.

1 tablespoon olive oil

2 portabello mushrooms, stem and gills removed

salt and freshly ground black pepper to taste

1 bakery loaf rye bread, unsliced

¾ cup Sir Kensington's Special Sauce (or thousand island dressing)

1 8 oz block of swiss cheese, thinly sliced.

1 cup sauerkraut, drained

In a small bowl, drizzle the olive oil over the portabello mushrooms, sprinkle with salt and pepper and toss to coat.

Grill the mushrooms on a portable campfire grill rack over hot coals for 5 minutes on each side. Remove from heat and place back in the bowl.

Cut the loaf of bread into 12, ¾ inch thick slices. Don't cut all the way through the bread though. Leave about ¼ inch of the bottom unsliced.

Spread the special sauce evenly over every other slice of bread. Evenly divide the cheese slices and stuff them into the sliced pockets of bread.

Thinly slice the mushrooms and along with the sauerkraut, evenly divide and stuff them into the bread pockets with the cheese.

Place the loaf on a large sheet of tinfoil then fold the edges around the loaf to seal. Cook on the grill rack for 15 minutes, turning several times, or until the cheese has melted and the loaf is hot.

Remove from heat, open the tinfoil, and allow it to sit for 5 minutes before serving.

SUGGESTED BEVERAGE: Easy Street Wheat – Odell Brewing Company (Ft. Collins, Colorado)

Tortilla española
Serves 2

I learned how to make this simple Spanish dish from a friend while living in Spain. I brought the recipe back to Colorado and this dish has become a staple for me both at home and camping.

¼ cup olive oil

1 large russet potato, diced into very small cubes

¼ cup yellow onion, diced

5 large eggs

salt to taste

¼ cup ketchup

¼ cup mayonnaise

hot sauce to taste

Heat the olive oil in a small skillet over hot coals or on a portable gas stove. Place the diced potato in a small bowl and cover with water. Allow it to sit for a few minutes then drain the water.
Add the potato to the skillet and sauté for about 10 minutes, stirring several times. Add the onion and cook 2 minutes longer.
While the potato mixture is cooking whisk the eggs in a large bowl. When the potatoes are soft, use a slotted spoon to scoop the potatoes and onions into the bowl with the eggs. Mix well to combine.
Pour the egg mixture back into the skillet, which should still have some olive oil in the bottom. Sprinkle on salt

to taste. Cook for about 5 minutes or until the eggs start to firm around the edges. Using a knife, separate the top side edges of the eggs from the pan. Place a plate, top side down, over the skillet and flip the skillet upside down, holding the plate tight against the top of the pan. The tortilla should fall out of the skillet onto the plate.

Return the skillet to the heat and push the tortilla, uncooked side down, back into the skillet. Cook for 5 minutes longer and remove from heat. Allow to cool for a few minutes then slice into pie shaped pieces. Serve warm.

For the dipping sauce mix equal parts ketchup and mayonnaise. Add a few dashes of hot sauce, stir and enjoy.

SUGGESTED BEVERAGE: Sangria - See *Colorado Peach Sangria.*

Samosa baked potatoes
Serves 2

This well seasoned baked potato features ginger and fresh garden cilantro, which seems to grow like weeds in my Denver garden. I pair the fresh cilantro with classic Indian spices which makes for a fantastic camping meal.

2 large baking potatoes

¼ cup olive oil

1 yellow onion, chopped

1 tablespoon minced fresh ginger

1 tablespoon curry powder

1 teaspoon brown mustard seeds

1 cup frozen or fresh peas

½ cup fresh cilantro, chopped

2 dollops plain greek yogurt

Wrap each potato separately in tinfoil and cook on hot coals in a campfire for about 1 hour, or until soft.
While the potatoes cook, heat the olive oil in a cast iron skillet and add the onion, ginger, curry powder and brown mustard seeds. Cook for 5 minutes, stirring often. Add the peas and cook for 3 minutes more. Remove the onion mixture from heat.
When the potatoes are done, remove from the fire and when cool enough to handle, cut lengthwise and place in bowls. Top each potato with half the onion mixture. Serve warm topped with cilantro and yogurt.

SUGGESTED BEVERAGE: Iced Tea - See *Wild Mint Sun Tea*.

Black-eyed pea sausage skillet supper
Serves 2

Black-eyed peas combine perfectly with cider vinegar, sausage and garden veggies in this simple skillet camping dish. I like to top it with a fried egg to complete the meal. You can easily substitute pork sausage for the elk if you prefer.

2 elk sausage links, thickly sliced

1 heirloom tomato, diced

1 celery stock, diced

1 red bell pepper, diced

1 yellow summer squash, diced

¼ cup water

3 teaspoons fresh thyme

3 teaspoons apple cider vinegar

2 teaspoons Worcestershire sauce

3 teaspoons Dijon mustard

1 tablespoon olive oil

1 15 oz can black-eyed peas

2 large eggs

freshly ground black pepper to taste

Heat a large cast iron skillet over a campfire. Add the sausages and sauté for about 5 minutes or until browned. Add the tomato, celery, red bell pepper and squash and sauté for about 4 minutes.

Add the water, thyme, vinegar, Worcestershire sauce, mustard, olive oil and peas. Simmer for 4 minutes or until the peas are warm. Remove the black-eyed pea mixture from the skillet and divide evenly in bowls.

Add some extra olive oil to the skillet and crack the eggs adding them to the skillet carefully. Cook for about 5 minutes or until the egg whites have set.

Remove the eggs from the campfire and top the pea mixture with 1 egg each. Sprinkle the eggs with black pepper and serve.

SUGGESTED BEVERAGE: Orchard Original Hard Cider – Big B's (Hotchkiss, Colorado)

Hobo chicken puttanesca

Serves 2

This easy foil packet meal cooks up an Italian inspired Colorado campfire dinner in no time. All you need is a few minutes of prep time and a nice hot campfire.

2 skinless, boneless chicken breasts, cubed

4 tablespoons olive oil

1 can artichoke hearts, drained

½ cup pitted kalamata olives

1 pint cherry tomatoes

2 tablespoons capers

5 cloves garlic, minced

¼ teaspoon red pepper flakes

salt and freshly ground black pepper to taste

1 small baguette

4 tablespoons Parmesan cheese

1 tablespoon fresh basil, chopped

At Home: Combine the chicken breast cubes, 2 tablespoons olive oil, artichoke hearts, olives, tomatoes, capers, 3 minced garlic cloves, red pepper flakes, salt and black pepper in a large plastic baggie. Seal and shake well to combine. Pack in a well iced cooler for camp.

At Camp: Evenly divide the chicken mixture on 2 large sheets of tinfoil. Fold up the sides of the tinfoil to form 2 sealed packets. Place the packets on hot coals in a campfire and cook for about 40 minutes or until the chicken is cooked through.

Meanwhile, combine the remaining olive oil, salt and garlic in a bowl. Cut the baguette in half then again in half lengthwise. Spread the olive oil mixture on the cut side of each baguette half. Sprinkle with Parmesan cheese. Toast the bread on a metal grate over the campfire. When golden brown remove from heat and sprinkle the basil on the bread.

Open the hobo packets and serve with toasted garlic bread.

SUGGESTED BEVERAGE: Red Wine Can – The Infinite Monkey Theorem (Denver, Colorado)

Campfire vampire steak

Serves 2

This steak features a garlic lover's marinade which sings when roasted over an open fire. Use Colorado beef for the best flavor.

5 garlic cloves, minced

½ lemon, juiced

2 teaspoons fresh tarragon, chopped

3 teaspoons smoked paprika

1 teaspoon dry parsley

1 flank steak, trimmed

salt and freshly ground black pepper to taste

At Home: Combine the garlic, lemon juice, tarragon, paprika and parsley in a bowl. Score a diamond pattern on both sides of the steak and rub the juice mixture evenly over both sides of the steak. Cover and store in a cooler for camp.

At Camp: Sprinkle salt and pepper evenly on both sides of the steak. Place the steak on a portable grill rack over the hot coals of a campfire. Grill for about 8 minutes on each side for medium.

Remove steak from grill and let stand for 5 minutes before cutting into thin slices.

Cut the steak across the grain and serve warm.

SUGGESTED BEVERAGE: Colorado Cabernet Franc - Balistreri Vineyard (Denver, Colorado)

Foraged mushroom tempeh kabobs
Serves 2

This asian inspired vegetarian dish is a great meat alternative for those looking for a good camping meal. The featured glaze is both sweet and salty.

5 teaspoons rice vinegar

1 teaspoon soy sauce

2 teaspoons toasted sesame oil

2 teaspoons red chile paste

1 teaspoon red pepper flakes

1 teaspoon freshly ground black pepper

1 8 oz package soy tempeh, cut into bite size pieces

2 tablespoons Colorado honey

1 tablespoon olive oil

1 lime, juiced

salt to taste

1 pint cherry tomatoes

1 large red bell pepper, cut into bit sized pieces

4 foraged Colorado mushrooms, such as the white Western Giant Puffball, quartered

At Home: Combine half the vinegar and the next 5 ingredients (through black pepper) in a large plastic baggie. Add the tempeh, seal and shake the ingredients well to combine. Let the tempeh marinate in a cooler on your way to camp. The longer it marinates the stronger the flavor will be.

At Camp: Combine the remaining vinegar, honey, olive oil, lime juice and salt in a small saucepan and cook over hot coals or a portable gas stove, simmering, for about 4 minutes or until the glaze thickens slightly.

Thread the cherry tomatoes, bell pepper, tempeh and mushrooms on skewers evenly alternating. Place the kabobs on a portable grill rack over hot coals and grill for about 5 minutes on each side.

While the kabobs cook, baste them with the honey glaze several times.

Remove from heat and drizzle any remaining honey glaze over the top of the kabobs. Serve warm.

SUGGESTED BEVERAGE: Iced Tea - See *Wild Mint Sun Tea*.

FORAGING TIPS: The rule with mushroom foraging is, if you don't know what it is or are not sure, don't eat it, so make sure you take care when selecting mushrooms. Western Giant Puffballs can be found at higher elevations most often in open fields. I have had the most luck finding this variety near sagebrush.

Colorado elk stroganoff
Serves 2

This easy camping recipe is great for featuring local Colorado elk. The mushrooms and herbs will fill your campsite with delicious smells as it simmers to perfection.

1 lb elk round steak

salt and freshly ground black pepper to taste

2 tablespoons olive oil

2 tablespoons Worcestershire sauce

1 tablespoon unsalted butter, plus 1 tablespoon for noodles

1 cup pearl onions

4 garlic cloves, minced

5 crimini mushrooms, or foraged mushrooms, sliced

1 tablespoon whole wheat flour

1 tablespoon fresh dill, chopped

1 tablespoon fresh thyme

¼ cup red wine

1 cup beef broth

¼ cup sour cream

1 package egg noodles

Slice the steak into thin strips and combine with salt, pepper, 1 tablespoon of the olive oil and Worcestershire sauce in a large plastic baggie. Seal, shake and allow the meat to marinate for about 40 minutes.

Heat a large cast iron skillet over hot coals or a portable gas stove. Add the butter and allow it to melt. Add the remaining olive oil and elk strips. Cook for about 4 minutes, turning to cook evenly on all sides. Remove the elk from heat and set aside.

Add the onions to the skillet and cook for 5 minutes or until they begin to brown. Add the garlic, mushrooms, flour, half the dill and half the thyme and stir to combine. Simmer for 2 minutes. Add the wine and scrape the bottom of the pan well to release the brown bits into the sauce.

Add the beef broth and simmer for 5 minutes. Add the sour cream and stir until combined. Stir in the remaining thyme and dill. Add the elk to the skillet again and cook for an additional 5 minutes.

Cook 1 package of egg noodles according to package directions. Use a Jetboil to boil the water or a sauce pan over hot coals or a gas stove. When the noodles are done chop 1 tablespoon of butter and stir into the hot noodles.

Pour the stroganoff over the top of the noodles and serve warm.

SUGGESTED BEVERAGE: Havin' a Cow Colorado Red Table Wine – Grande River Vineyards (Palisade, Colorado)

Colorado pesto mushroom sandwiches
Serves 2

This meal requires foraging for the ingredients but it is incredibly worth the work. It features foraged Colorado mushrooms and pesto made from wild bergamot or bee balm. Note that you will need to bring a manual food processor with you to make the pesto. If you would rather bring store bought pesto and enjoy it with foraged Colorado mushrooms you can certainly do that as well.

1 ½ cups olive oil

2 cups foraged Colorado mushrooms such as chanterelles

freshly ground black pepper to taste

2 ½ cups arugula

2 cups wild bergamot

2 garlic cloves

½ cup pine nuts

½ cup Pecorino Romano cheese, grated

salt to taste

1 fresh baguette halved lengthwise

Heat a large cast iron skillet over hot coals or a portable gas stove and add ½ cup of the olive oil to the skillet. Slice the foraged mushrooms and add them to the olive oil. Sauté for 8 minutes or until browned. Sprinkle with black pepper and remove from heat.

While the mushrooms cook, combine the arugula, wild

bergamot, garlic cloves, pine nuts, cheese, remaining olive oil and salt in a manual food processor. Crank the handle until coarsely chopped.

Spread the pesto evenly on both sides of the sliced baguette and top with the sautéd mushrooms.

Serve warm.

SUGGESTED BEVERAGE: Peach Beer - See *Honey Palisade Peach Beer.*

FORAGING TIPS: Chanterelles can be found in forested areas, especially in aspen groves anywhere from 7,000 to 11,000 feet in elevation. Exercise extreme caution with chanterelles as there are some mushroom varieties that look similar but can leave you very sick. Examine the chanterelle gills which are false. This means they should not be separate but one mass. You can find them from summer to early fall. Wild bergamot can be found on dry hillsides from 7,000 to 8,000 feet in elevation. This delicious wild plant is similar in flavor to oregano.

Wild dandelion greens salad

Serves 4

Dandelions are abundant in the mountains and easily found near campsites. The leaves also happen to be quite tasty, are great for your health and make an excellent fresh salad that you don't have to pack.

1 tablespoon lemon juice

salt to taste

¼ teaspoon sugar

¼ cup olive oil

3 cups foraged dandelion greens

3 wild spring garlic, minced

In a large bowl whisk the lemon juice, salt, sugar and olive oil until emulsified.
Add the dandelion greens and garlic to the bowl and mix well before serving.

FORAGING TIPS: Dandelion greens are arguably the most abundant and most easily identifiable foraged vegetable anywhere in Colorado. They are not only abundant but also really good for you. Be sure to wash them well before eating and avoid harvesting greens from anywhere that has been sprayed with weed killer. You can easily find them near most campsites in Colorado. They can be found throughout the summer. Try to avoid dandelions that have gone to flower because their leaves will be more bitter.

Bacon campfire potato with wild onions
Serves 2

This recipe could easily be made as a simple main dish, but it goes great with burgers, sausages or whatever you might be cooking on the fire. Start cooking these potatoes before everything else, as it takes a while.

2 large russet potatoes

1 bacon slice

2 tablespoons butter

salt and freshly ground black pepper to taste

½ cup foraged wild onions, chopped

Using 2 large sheets of tinfoil, form 2 pockets. Poke a few holes in the potatoes with a fork and place them each on a tinfoil sheet.

Place half a slice of bacon and 1 tablespoon of butter on top of each potato. As it cooks you want to make sure the butter melts down the sides of the potato.

Sprinkle with salt and pepper and enclose completely in the tinfoil. Place the package, butter side up, on hot coals in the fire and cook for 45 minutes to an hour.

When done, sprinkle fresh wild onions on top of each potato.

FORAGING TIPS: Wild onions can be found in early spring and are abundant until late fall. They have wide flat green leaves and are most easily identifiable by a strong onion smell. They look similar to a poisonous plant called *death camas* so use caution. When bloomed the onion has pink flowers and *death camas* have white flowers, which makes it easy to tell them apart. You can find wild onions all over Colorado, especially in moist meadows and on hillsides.

Cilantro lime olathe sweet corn
Serves 4

Growing up I would inevitably make it to the Olathe Sweet Corn Festival each August to enjoy the local corn harvest cooked in every way imaginable. You will start to see this Colorado gem in late July. Snatch it up while you can and enjoy this recipe fireside.

4 ears Olathe sweet corn, husked

2 tablespoons butter

1 lime, juiced

1 tablespoon fresh cilantro, chopped

salt and freshly ground black pepper to taste

¼ cup crumbled feta cheese

Place the corn on individual sheets of aluminum foil. Divided evenly between the 4 ears of corn, top with butter, lime juice, cilantro, salt, pepper and crumbled feta cheese.

Tightly roll the foil around the corn and make sure it is sealed. Cook over hot campfire coals for about 5 minutes on each side.

Remove from fire, unwrap and serve immediately.

Dutch oven baked beans

Serves 4

Beans seem to be the perfect outdoor side dish. Traditionally they are served alongside grilled meats. These beans are loaded with flavor and often steal the show from your main.

1 tablespoon olive oil

2 slices thick cut bacon, cut in half

1 yellow onion, chopped

1 garlic clove, minced

2 cans navy beans, undrained

1 cup water

1 cup brown sugar

¼ cup molasses

¼ cup BBQ sauce

1 dash Worcestershire sauce

1 teaspoon freshly ground black pepper

½ teaspoon dry mustard

¼ teaspoon garlic powder

Heat the olive oil in a dutch oven over hot coals over a campfire. Add the bacon and cook for 5 minutes or until the drippings start to release into the pan. Add the onion and garlic and sauté with the bacon for 3 minutes.

Add the rest of the ingredients and simmer uncovered for 20 minutes or until the sauce is thick.

Serve warm.

Wild onion potato salad
Serves 4

I like using fingerling potatoes because they cook faster. The thing that makes this dish special is the wild onions which seem to be everywhere in the the spring. Wild onions, just chopped from a field or your garden have such a wonderful and intense flavor that really adds to this tangy ranch flavored side.

1 teaspoon pink Himalayan salt

2 lbs fingerling potatoes

¼ cup plain whole milk yogurt

1 tablespoon Dijon mustard

½ lemon juiced

1 teaspoon freshly ground black pepper

½ teaspoon honey

2 garlic cloves, minced

½ cup celery, chopped

3 tablespoons fresh dill, chopped

½ red bell pepper, chopped

1 cup chopped fresh wild onions

At Home: Bring a pot of water to a boil, adding a pinch of salt. Cut the fingerling potatoes in half and add them to the water, which should cover the potatoes. Simmer for about 25 minutes or until you poke them with a fork and they are soft. Drain and rinse with cold water. Combine the yogurt, mustard, lemon juice, pepper, honey and garlic in a large bowl stirring well. Add the potatoes, celery, dill and bell pepper, stirring to ensure everything is coated in the yogurt mixture.

Pack the potato salad in tupperware and store in a cooler for camp.

At Camp: Forage for wild onions and add to the top of the potato salad before serving.

FORAGING TIPS: Wild onions can be found in early spring and are abundant until late fall. They have wide flat green leaves and are most easily identifiable by a strong onion smell. They look similar to a poisonous plant called *death camas* so use caution. When bloomed the onion has pink flowers and *death camas* have white flowers, which makes it easy to tell them apart. You can find wild onions all over Colorado, especially in moist meadows and on hillsides.

Fireside feta with thyme
Serves 4

Grilling cheese imparts a smokey layer of flavor that is irresistible. If you are looking for a side or even a quick appetizer that is both gourmet and easy, look no further. If you have access to an outdoor grill, you can use that as well, but I prefer to make this over a campfire.

1 medium block of feta cheese

8 sprigs fresh thyme

freshly ground black pepper

3 tablespoons olive oil

1 package pita bread

Let the cheese warm to outside temperature as you prepare your campfire. Place a portable grill rack over hot coals and place the block of cheese in the center of a sheet of tinfoil.

Top the cheese with thyme, pepper and olive oil and wrap with the tinfoil, sealing to make a foil packet. Place the packet on the grill and allow it to cook for about 10 minutes.

Remove from heat, open the packet, making sure not to spill the oils and liquid in the foil. Remove the cheese from the foil and place the cheese back on the grill, cooking for 2 minutes on both long sides, or until you see grill marks. Remove the cheese from heat, place in a shallow bowl and pour the olive oil and

thyme mixture over the top of the feta.
Brush the pita bread with olive oil and grill for 2 minutes on each side, until crisp.
Serve the pita bread warm with the cheese and oil.

Colorado cantaloupe and prosciutto salad

Serves 2

Colorado grows some tasty cantaloupe which you will begin to see in farmers markets and grocery stores in July. This makes a tasty, fresh, local and easy side for camping.

2 tablespoons olive oil

1 teaspoon sherry vinegar

2 cups arugula or foraged dandelion greens

1 cantaloupe, for example from Rocky Ford, peeled, seeded and cut lengthwise into wedges

3 slices prosciutto

¾ cup crumbled blue cheese

1 tablespoon honey

salt and freshly ground black pepper to taste

In a bowl combine 1 tablespoon of the oil and all of the vinegar with a whisk or fork until emulsified. Add the arugula to the bowl and toss to coat with the oil mixture.

Place 4 cantaloupe wedges on a plate for each serving. Top the cantaloupe with ½ of the arugula mixture, followed by ½ of the prosciutto and ½ of the blue cheese. Drizzle the remaining olive oil and honey over the salad. Sprinkle with salt and pepper.

Serve cold.

Skillet mac and cheese crisp
Serves 4

Who doesn't love mac and cheese? This dish goes great with grilled meats and tastes amazing cooked in a cast iron skillet over an open flame.

1 lb box of elbow pasta

4 tablespoons Parmesan cheese, grated

3 tablespoons all purpose flour

3 cups whole milk

2 cups shredded sharp cheddar cheese

2 teaspoons mustard powder

1 teaspoon smoked paprika

¼ teaspoon cayenne pepper

¼ teaspoon salt

Bring a pot of salted water to a boil using a portable gas cooking stove or very hot coals. Cook the pasta according to package directions. I recommend using white flour pasta instead of whole wheat while camping because it takes less time to cook.

While the pasta cooks, heat a cast iron skillet over hot coals and add the Parmesan to the pan. Using a spatula, quickly bunch the cheese together and flatten into a thin layer. Allow the cheese to melt together, forming a disk, and cook for 2 minutes. Flip and cook for 2 more minutes or until crispy golden brown. Remove the crisp from the pan and set on a paper towel.

In the skillet, whisk the flour into the milk and bring it to a simmer, stirring often. Simmer for 3 – 4 minutes or until it thickens slightly. Stir in the cheddar cheese, mustard powder, paprika, cayenne and salt. Whisk until smooth and simmer for 1 minute.

Add the cooked pasta to the skillet and stir to combine with the sauce. Cook over hot coals for 5 minutes or until heated though.

Serve hot with cheese crisps on top.

Campfire jalapeño poppers
Serves 6

Jalapeño poppers are one of my favorite all time things to eat no matter the type of gathering. If you are camping with a large group, make these delicious, spicy and cheesy poppers over the campfire and impress your camping buddies.

½ cup goat cheese

1 cup cream cheese

2 tablespoons green onions, thinly sliced

½ teaspoon salt

2 tablespoons fresh sage, chopped

14 jalapeño peppers, halved lengthwise and seeded

2 tablespoons fresh cilantro, chopped

At Home: Combine the goat cheese, cream cheese, onions, salt, and sage in a bowl. Store in a large plastic baggie and store in a cooler for camp.

At Camp: Place a portable grill rack over the hot coals of a campfire. Spoon about 1 tablespoon of the cheese mixture into each pepper half. Place the pepper halves, cheese side up on the grill and cook for 7 minutes, or until the bottoms of the peppers are charred and the cheese mixture is slightly browned.

Remove from heat, sprinkle the cilantro on top of the peppers and serve warm.

Garlic baby broccoli
Serves 4

This simple side dish is perfect for garlic lovers. If a dish is meat heavy I like to pair it with a vegetable on the side and this broccoli recipe is one of my favorites.

½ cup olive oil

8 garlic cloves, sliced

1 lb baby broccoli, ends trimmed

1 teaspoon crushed red pepper flakes
salt to taste

Heat the olive oil in a large cast iron skillet over a campfire or portable gas stove. Add the garlic first, then the broccoli, followed by the red pepper flakes.
Sauté for 10 minutes, flipping the broccoli several times, until the broccoli has wilted and begins to brown. Sprinkle with salt and remove from heat.
Serve warm with bits of garlic and olive oil drizzled over the top.

Grilled palisade peach salad with goat cheese
Serves 4

Palisade peaches are one of my favorite local Colorado ingredients to use during the summer. Ask local chefs and they will tell you the same thing. This recipe is simple and captures the Colorado summer on a plate. You should start to see Palisade peaches in stores and farmers markets beginning in late July.

4 Palisade peaches, pitted and halved

1 lemon, juiced

½ cup olive oil

freshly ground black pepper to taste

1 head red leaf lettuce, rinsed and chopped

1 7 oz package local Haystack Mountain Goat Cheese, such as Snowdrop

Place a portable grill rack over a fire or hot coals and place the peaches, cut side down on the grill. Allow them to cook for 6 – 8 minutes then flip and grill 5 minutes more. They should start to break down and get grill marks on both sides.

While the peaches cook, whisk the lemon juice, olive oil and pepper in a large bowl. Add the lettuce and toss to coat.

Thinly slice the goat cheese and set aside. Make a bed of the lettuce mixture, evenly divided, between 4 plates. Top each with grilled peach halves, cut side up and top the peaches with goat cheese.

Serve while the peaches are still warm for the best

flavor.

3 bean salad

Serves 4

This dish features apple cider vinegar which is my favorite vinegar to use during the summer. It pairs well with grilled meats and goes great with beans. I usually make this at home and store it in my cooler, but you can easily make this at camp as well if you prefer.

- 2 tablespoons olive oil
- 2 tablespoons apple cider vinegar
- 1 lime, juiced
- 1 tablespoon honey
- 1 8.5 oz can garbanzo beans, drained and rinsed
- 1 8.5 oz can black beans, drained and rinsed
- 1 8.5 oz can red kidney beans, drained and rinsed
- 1 red bell pepper, chopped
- ½ cup red onion, chopped
- ½ cup cilantro
- 1 teaspoon cumin
- 1 teaspoon chili powder
- 1 garlic clove minced
- salt and freshly ground black pepper to taste

At Home: In a large bowl whisk the olive oil, vinegar, lime juice and honey until well combined. Add the rest of the ingredients and fold together to combine. Store in a large tupperware container in a cooler for camp.

This dish will taste best if it is allowed to chill for a few hours so if you decide to make it at camp, put it in the cooler for a while to let the flavors marinate.
Toss gently before serving.

Heirloom carrot and apple slaw

Serves 4

Colorful heirloom carrots grow great in Colorado gardens and when I pick them from my garden, some purple, yellow and of course orange, they have almost a hint of apple flavor in them. Perhaps that is why they pair so well with Colorado apples in this quick side that goes great with any barbecue.

½ cup Greek yogurt

2 tablespoons white wine vinegar

salt and freshly ground black pepper to taste

½ teaspoon ground cumin

4 multicolored carrots, grated

1 tart Colorado apple, cored and grated

¼ cup fresh cilantro, chopped

½ cup golden raisins

Whisk together the yogurt, vinegar, salt, pepper and cumin in a large bowl. Add the grated carrots, apple, cilantro and raisins to the bowl and stir well to combine.
Serve cold.

Black-eyed pea summer salad
Serves 4

This is probably my favorite thing to eat during the summer. I love vinegar, which is prominent in this dish. This is a side that is hearty enough to be eaten as a light main or for lunch with some pita bread or chips.

2 tablespoons apple cider vinegar

1 teaspoon ground cumin

3 tablespoons olive oil

salt and freshly ground black pepper to taste

1 8.5 oz can of black-eyed peas, drained

1 jalapeño, seeded and diced

1 pint cherry tomatoes, chopped

¼ red onion, chopped

1 red bell pepper, seeded and chopped

1 avocado, sliced

In a large bowl, whisk together the vinegar, cumin, olive oil, salt and pepper.
Add the black-eyed peas, jalapeño, tomatoes, onion and bell pepper, mixing well to combine.
Serve cold with avocado slices on top.

Goat cheese pasta salad with basil oil
Serves 4

If you like basil, then you will love this simple side. Make it ahead of time, and enjoy it on the side of grilled meats or even as a light main. I like to make it with whole wheat pasta and local Haystack Farms goat cheese to make it extra healthy and tasty.

1 lb penne or fusilli pasta

2 ½ cups fresh basil

½ cup olive oil

4 oz goat cheese

½ teaspoon salt

¼ teaspoon freshly ground black pepper

At Home: Cook the pasta in boiling water according to package directions, drain and return to the pot.

While the pasta cooks, puree 2 cups of the basil and all of the olive oil in a blender until smooth. Toss the pasta with the basil puree, goat cheese, ½ cup additional basil leaves, salt and pepper.

Store in a large tupperware container and pack in a cooler for camp. Serve at room temperature.

Summer squash gremolata
Serves 4

Grilled to perfection, this easy side goes great with just about anything you are cooking for dinner. I particularly enjoy it with steaks or grilled chicken.

2 tablespoons fresh parsley, chopped

½ lemon, juiced

1 ½ teaspoons olive oil

½ teaspoon salt

½ teaspoon freshly ground black pepper

2 garlic cloves, minced

3 yellow squash, cut lengthwise into 4 long slices each

Combine the parsley, lemon juice, olive oil, salt, pepper and garlic in a large bowl.

Rub extra olive oil on the squash slices to coat and skewer them on several green campfire sticks. Cook over hot coals for about 5 minutes, rotating slowly. If you prefer, you could also cook them on a portable campfire grill rack instead.

Add the squash to the parsley mixture and toss gently to coat.

Serve warm.

Pimientos de padrón
Serves 2

I first had pimientos de padrón in Northwest Spain and promptly planted these peppers in my Colorado garden when I got home. They can be hard to find in stores, so use shishito peppers, which are much easier to come by, if you can't find or grow pimientos de padrón yourself. Today, many Colorado restaurants are serving a version of this simple dish.

½ cup olive oil

15 pimientos de padrón or shishito peppers

kosher salt to taste

Heat the oil in a large cast iron skillet over hot coals or on a portable gas stove. When the oil is hot, add the peppers, whole, to the pan, turning a few times until the skin begins to blister and a they just begin to char. Remove from heat and serve warm on a plate, sprinkled with a liberal amount of salt.

Pear prosciutto and wild dandelion green bites
Serves 4

Fall brings delicious pears to the orchards around Colorado and once you get your hands on some, this makes a light side that is much fancier than it is difficult to prepare.

1 Colorado pear, cut into 8 wedges

1 teaspoon fresh lemon juice

8 foraged dandelion green leaves

2 oz blue cheese crumbles

8 thin slices prosciutto

In a small bowl, toss the pear wedges with the lemon juice. Place a few blue cheese crumbles on each pear and then a dandelion green on top of the blue cheese. Wrap everything with a piece of prosciutto so all the ingredients are held together.

Serve at room temperature.

FORAGING TIPS: Dandelion greens are arguably the most abundant and most easily identifiable foraged vegetable anywhere in Colorado. They are not only abundant but also really good for you. Be sure to wash them well before eating and avoid harvesting greens from anywhere that has been sprayed with weed killer. You can easily find them near most campsites in Colorado. They can be found throughout the summer. Try to avoid dandelions that have gone to flower because their leaves will be more bitter.

Pickled slaw
Serves 4

Have you ever taken a swig of pickle juice, just because you love pickles so much? If so, you love all things pickles as much as I do. This quick slaw goes great with grilled meats and satisfies your pickle tooth. This can easily be made ahead and stored in a cooler or made at camp if you prefer.

1 head red cabbage, cored and sliced into thin ribbons

1 head green cabbage, cored and sliced into thin ribbons

2 tart apples, cut into matchsticks

2 carrots, grated

½ cup mayonnaise

5 tablespoons pickle juice

1 tablespoon Dijon mustard

1 tablespoon apple cider vinegar

1 teaspoon hot sauce

salt and freshly ground black pepper to taste

In a large bowl, mix the cabbage, apples and carrots.
In a separate bowl, whisk together the mayonnaise, pickle juice, mustard, vinegar, hot sauce, salt and pepper.
Pour the pickle juice mixture over the top of the vegetable mixture and toss to combine. You can serve immediately or allow it to marinate for up to a day.
Serve cold.

Cucumber lime salad
Serves 4

This refreshing summer salad is perfect for any camping trip. It offers a nice refreshing kick. I like to make this ahead of time at home and pack it in the cooler, but you can also make it fresh at camp.

3 garlic cloves, minced

1 jalapeño, seeded and minced

2 limes, juiced

3 tablespoons olive oil

¼ teaspoon crushed red pepper

salt and freshly ground black pepper to taste

2 cucumbers, thinly sliced

2 tablespoons cilantro, chopped

In a large bowl whisk together the garlic, jalapeño, lime juice, olive oil, red pepper, salt and black pepper.
Add the cucumbers to the dressing and toss to coat. Add the cilantro, stir to combine and either pack for camp, which allows for some great marination time, or serve fresh.

Flame kissed watermelon salad
Serves 4

Cooking chunks of watermelons, like marshmallows, on a stick over the campfire will make perfect sense after you taste this wonderful summer salad.

2 tablespoons sherry vinegar

1 small red onion, sliced

½ small watermelon, cut into large marshmallow sized cubes

3 tablespoons olive oil

salt to taste

1 tablespoon foraged wild mint, or store bought

1 cup crumbled feta cheese

¼ teaspoon chili powder

In a large bowl combine the vinegar and red onion, and let the onion marinate for 10 minutes. Drain and place the onions on a paper towel to dry.

Brush the watermelons with olive oil and skewer on the end of a green campfire stick. Cook over campfire coals, rotating slowly as you would a marshmallow, for about 10 minutes, or until the watermelon begins to char.

Remove from the fire and add the watermelon to a large bowl. Add the onions to the watermelon chunks, along with the remaining ingredients and toss to combine.

Serve while the watermelon is still slightly warm.

FORAGING TIPS: An easily recognizable ingredient, mint grows wild in most areas of Colorado, especially if you are camping near water. Wild mint begins to bloom from June to October and can be found from low to moderate elevations.

Cider vinegar baby spinach
Serves 2

This simple tangy side dish goes great with barbecued meats and only takes a few minutes to prepare. I like to prepare this dish when the main takes up more of my cooking time.

1 tablespoon water

1 5 oz package, pre-washed baby spinach

3 tablespoons apple cider vinegar

¼ teaspoon crushed red pepper

¼ teaspoon freshly ground black pepper

pinch of salt

Heat the water in a medium sized skillet over hot coals or a portable gas stove. When the water begins to simmer add the spinach, cover and cook for about 5 minutes or until the spinach begins to wilt.
Drain any excess water from the skillet and add the remaining ingredients, stirring well to combine.
Serve warm.

Olathe sweet corn bread
Serves 2

This corn bread is cooked in a cast iron skillet and features local Olathe sweet corn. This recipe can be a little more complicated than I like for a camping side but it is always worth the effort.

1 cup yellow cornmeal

¼ cup flour

1 tablespoon baking powder

1 teaspoon salt

1 teaspoon freshly ground black pepper

¼ cup Olathe sweet corn kernels, cut fresh from the cob

1 large egg

1 cup milk

2 tablespoons honey

½ tablespoon olive oil

Mix the cornmeal, flour, baking powder, salt and pepper together in a large bowl. Add the corn kernels, egg, milk and honey to the bowl and mix well.

Heat the olive oil in a cast iron skillet over hot campfire coals. Swirl the oil in the pan to coat and pour the cornmeal batter into the skillet. Cover the skillet with tinfoil and cook over the campfire for about 18 minutes. Remove from heat, leave the cover on, and let it sit for an additional 5-8 minutes.

Remove the cover, cut and serve warm with some

extra honey drizzled over the top.

Halloumi vegetable skewers
Serves 2

Cheese cooked over open flames is made possible by halloumi, which can hold up well without melting into a glob. Cooked with summer garden vegetables, common in Colorado, this side is a delight.

1 8 oz block halloumi cheese, cut into large 1 inch chunks

1 tablespoon olive oil

½ cup heirloom cherry tomatoes

1 zucchini, cut into 1 inch slices

1 yellow onion, quartered

1 red bell pepper, seeded and cut into 1 inch chunks

salt and freshly ground black pepper to taste

In a large bowl combine all of the ingredients and stir well to coat evenly with the olive oil.

Alternate cheese, tomatoes, zucchini, onion and bell pepper, threading them onto either bamboo skewer sticks or a green campfire stick, until there is no room left on the stick.

Repeat until all of your ingredients are ready for the fire. Cook over hot coals, rotating to cook evenly, for about 10 minutes, or until the tomatoes begin to break down and the cheese is golden brown.

Remove the ingredients from the sticks and serve warm.

Quinoa with fresh herbs

Serves 4

For this recipe I like to use whatever herbs are ready in my summer garden or that I can buy at the farmers market. Feel free to swap the herbs I use for what you have on hand. I like to make this recipe at home and then pack it for camp. The extra time spent in the cooler seems to allow the flavors to mingle and intensify.

2 tablespoons olive oil

½ small yellow onion, chopped

2 garlic cloves, minced

1 ½ cups quinoa, rinsed

2 cups water

salt to taste

½ cup kalamata olives, pitted and chopped

½ cup pine nuts

½ cup fresh basil, chopped

¼ cup parsley, chopped

¼ cup fresh cilantro, chopped

At Home: Heat the olive oil in a large sauce pan over medium heat. Add the onion and sauté until soft, about 5 minutes. Add the garlic and cook for 1 minute more. Add the quinoa and cook for 1 minute.

Add the water, season with salt and simmer, covered, until the water is absorbed, about 17 minutes. Remove from heat and let stand for 5 minutes.

Add the olives, pine nuts, basil, parsley, and cilantro, tossing well to combine. Season with more salt. Pack in tupperware and store in a cooler for camp.
Serve at room temperature.

I love dessert and tend to make s'mores most often while camping. Who doesn't love marshmallows roasted over hot coals in a campfire? But there are so many yummy fire roasted desserts to try at least once on your next camping trip.

My recipes use less sugar than is typical as I don't like overly sweet treats and the desserts listed here tend to lean this direction. I like to let the local Colorado ingredients shine and it is best not to get in the way of a Colorado peach, cherry, apricot or apple.

After a day of exploring the outdoors and cooking a full meal for dinner, I want my dessert to be both easy and delicious, so most of these recipes are very simple and easy to prepare.

You will need some basic cooking equipment to prepare the dessert recipes listed. These include:
- Large Mixing Bowl
- Sharp Knife
- Tinfoil

- Portable Gas Stove (if you prefer not to cook over a fire)
- Dutch Oven / Large Cast Iron Skillet
- Pie Iron
  Some of the recipes listed, such as the homemade marshmallows, are best made in the home kitchen and then packed for camp.

Pie iron apple pie
Serves 4

You will need a pie iron for this recipe. If you don't already have a pie iron they are inexpensive and available almost everywhere camping goods are sold. If you don't want to own a pie iron simply make the pie filling for this recipe and serve topped with fresh whipped cream and cinnamon graham crackers.

3 tablespoons unsalted butter

1 teaspoon cinnamon

4 medium Colorado apples, peeled, cored and sliced

¼ cup sugar

5 tablespoons water

1 tablespoon plus 1 teaspoon cornstarch

brown sugar to taste

1 loaf honey whole wheat bread, sliced

In a large saucepan or skillet, heat 2 tablespoons butter and cinnamon. Stir in apples, sugar and 3 tablespoons of water. Cover and cook, stirring occasionally for 7 minutes, or until the apples begin to soften.

In a small bowl combine cornstarch and 2 tablespoons of water. Add the cornstarch mix to the pan while stirring and cook for an additional 5 minutes or until the filling thickens.

Remove from heat and cool to mountain air temperature.

Meanwhile, heat the pie irons over hot coals and rub

the inside with remaining butter. Sprinkle brown sugar on the insides of the pie irons.

Place 1 slice of bread on 1 side of the iron, top with a spoonful of apple pie filling. Sprinkle with some brown sugar and extra cinnamon to taste. Place a second slice of bread on top and close the pie iron.

Hold the iron over the campfire for 2 minutes, flip, and hold over the fire for 2 minutes more.

Open the pie iron and serve warm.

Banana boats
Serves 4

If you have never tried a banana boat it is high time you got on board. I make this dessert almost every camping trip because they are easy, fun and a delicious way to end a meal.

4 bananas

½ cup mini marshmallows

1 cup dark chocolate chips

Cut each banana lengthwise about halfway through the center of the banana, making sure not to slice all the way through. You want the banana to act as a hot dog bun, or a boat, able to hold the ingredients in the middle.

Stuff each banana with evenly divided marshmallows and chocolate chips.

Wrap each banana boat in tinfoil, sealing each to form a packet. Add the packets to hot coals and cook for about 10 minutes, or until the chocolate has completely melted and the banana has softened.

Serve warm.

Colorado s'mores
Serves 4

There is no more classic camping dessert than s'mores. This gourmet version incorporates some delicious local Colorado produce which peaks at the height of the sweet summer.

4 marshmallows

1 cup Colorado cherries, pitted and cut in half

1 bar of dark chocolate

4 graham crackers

Using a green stick, sharpened at the end to roast the marshmallows over the campfire for 5 minutes or until golden brown and gooey in the center.

Working quickly, break 1 graham cracker in half and place 2 pieces of dark chocolate on 1 halved graham cracker. Top with 4 cherry halves and the still warm marshmallow. Enclose with the other graham cracker half and squeeze so the marshmallow touches the chocolate, allowing it to melt slightly.

Serve warm.

Dutch oven peach cobbler

Serves 4

Summer in Colorado brings, in my opinion, the best juicy local peaches in the world. Eating a just picked peach alone is a satisfying dessert, but if you want something slightly more exciting, try this easy dish.

4 Colorado peaches, sliced

1 package yellow cake mix

1 stick of butter, sliced

½ cup pecans, chopped

Cut the peaches over your skillet, allowing all of the dripping juices to collect in the pan. Spread the peaches evenly over the bottom of the skillet.

Sprinkle the cake mixture over the top of the peaches. Cut pieces of butter and space evenly on top of the cake mixture, then sprinkle evenly with the pecans.

Cover the dutch oven and cook over hot coals for 45 minutes, or until the cake mix is light brown.

Serve warm.

Dulce de leche apricot kebobs
Serves 4

As a kid growing up in Colorado, we had an apricot tree growing in our front yard. Allowed to ripen on the tree, apricots make an exciting dessert, especially when roasted and paired with marshmallows and dulce de leche.

8 apricots, pitted and cut in half

8 marshmallows

1 jar dulce de leche

Using either a fresh green stick or kabob skewers thread the apricot halves and marshmallows alternately on the skewers.

Roast over hot coals for 8 – 10 minutes, rotating several times to evenly roast on all sides. The marshmallows should be golden brown.

Remove from heat and use a spoon to drizzle dulce de leche over the top of the kabobs.

Serve warm.

Salty peanut butter chocolate s'mores
Serves 4

This twist on a classic s'more is perfect for those who love salty and sweet combined. I adore peanut butter cups and this is a perfect way to jazz them up while camping.

4 marshmallows

4 peanut butter cups

8 Late July Classic Rich crackers, or Ritz crackers

Using a green stick, sharpened at the end, roast the marshmallows over a campfire for 5 minutes or until golden brown and gooey in the center.

Working quickly, place a peanut butter cup on a cracker. Top with a still warm marshmallow. Enclose with the other cracker half and squeeze so the marshmallow touches the peanut butter cup, allowing it to melt slightly.

Serve warm.

Conclusion

Managing food outdoors can be quite daunting. There's so much you have to look out for and if you forget a single food item, your whole meal experience can come tumbling down in blink. It is always a good idea to make a list prior to the trip and keep the backpacks ready beforehand to avoid any eleventh hour hassle.

I hope you will enjoy these recipes and have an amazing camping experience. Please feel free to share your experience camping with this cookbook writing an Amazon review, it would be very helpful and interesting to read.

Part 2

Introduction

My first experiences cooking in the great outdoors were with my family in the mountains near Crested Butte, Colorado. We would carve long green sticks to ready them for cooking and enjoy hot dogs, s'mores and all kinds of delicious food, which always tasted better outside. As I grew up, I transitioned from being fed to being the cook and a love for cooking at home boiled over to creating memorable camping meals.

I was born on the western slope of Colorado and grew up surrounded by cherries, peaches, sweet corn and more. I remember the seasons based on what was available and ripe for the picking both in the mountains and in farmers markets. Growing up in a small town, surrounded by orchards, taught me the joy of eating what was in season and my cooking today reflects this passion.

My first experience with foraging for food was when my neighbor, Dixie, asked my mom and I to bring her back a box full of chokecherries from the mountains. She wanted to make chokecherry jam and promised a few jars as a reward. As I discovered the abundance of this fruit in the mountains I began to ask myself, what else can you eat here in the wild? We filled a cardboard box full of chokecherries and the thrill of harvesting food that tastes better than the stuff you can find in supermarkets stayed with me. The adventurous flavors of foraged Colorado food began to make their way into my recipes.

Today, when I find something delicious, I work to feature it that night, cooked over the open flames of a campfire or enjoyed in a drink.
The dishes in this cookbook feature the best local ingredients that Colorado has to offer, including wild chokecherry jam. Coloradans are lucky to live in a state that provides some of the best ingredients around. Combine this great bounty with a campfire and you have a recipe for success.

C Lazy U "Woodsie" Trout Breakfast

»–Serves 4–»

This recipe comes from the talented Dennis Kaniger, the executive chef at C Lazy U Ranch near Granby, Colorado. Dennis prepares this "woodsie" outdoor breakfast for ranch guests during the summer months as they watch moose meander through Willow Creek and pronghorn heading up Mount Baldy. To me, fresh trout tastes like Colorado, and this recipe , served with cottage fried potatoes, bacon and links is the perfect way to start your Colorado day.

2 large Russet potatoes, diced

2 tablespoons unsalted butter

1 Spanish onion, diced

1 green bell pepper, diced

salt and freshly ground black pepper to taste

1 tablespoon paprika

¾ cup fresh parsley, chopped

8 strips thick-cut rashers apple wood smoked bacon

8 Italian breakfast link sausages

4 fresh Colorado river brook trout, filleted and butterflied

At Home: At C Lazy U Ranch, before they head up to the cook site, they do some prep before hand, which is what I like to do as well.

Blanch the diced potatoes in a pot of boiling salted water until they are halfway cooked, about 5 minutes.

Pack the rest of your ingredients, along with the blanched potatoes in a cooler.

At Camp: C Lazy U uses a heavy steel griddle fired by coal, but you can get a good campfire going as well and place a griddle, or large cast iron skillet over the hot coals.

Add the butter, potatoes, onions and peppers to the griddle and cook until the vegetables start to brown.

Season the potatoes with salt, pepper, paprika and parsley.

Start cooking the bacon and sausages until they are brown and crispy. As the meats cook sprinkle a touch of salt and pepper on the inside of the trout filets. Remove the bacon and sausage from the griddle and cook the trout, flesh side down, in the bacon fat, just until golden, no more than 3 minutes. Flip them over to the skin side, and crisp the skin. Another 3 – 4 minutes.

Serve the potatoes, bacon, links and trout on a large plate.
SUGGESTED BEVERAGE: Hot coffee. See The Best Camping Coffee In The World.

Honey Sweet Potato Breakfast Burritos

»–Serves 4–»

A late morning spent sitting outside, preparing for a hike through the Rocky Mountains calls for a hearty and delicious breakfast. These hearty vegetarian breakfast burritos have a unique flavor that I love and will keep you fueled through a long hike.

1 large sweet potato, diced into small cubes

2 tablespoons of olive oil

dash cayenne pepper

salt and freshly ground black pepper to taste

1 small sweet yellow onion, diced

1 clove of garlic, minced

4 eggs

½ cup feta cheese

1 tablespoon honey

4 large flour tortillas

At Home: Preheat the oven to 400 degrees. Spread the diced sweet potatoes onto a large baking sheet. Pour 1 tablespoon of the olive oil over the sweet potatoes and sprinkle with the cayenne pepper, salt and black pepper. Mix the potatoes to thoroughly coat with the olive oil and spices. Bake at 400 degrees for 40 minutes.

Remove from heat and let cool to room temperature. Store the potatoes in tupperware and pack in a cooler for camp.

At Camp: Heat 1 tablespoon of olive oil in a large cast iron skillet and add the yellow onion. Sauté for 5 minutes then add garlic and cook for 1 minute more. Add the eggs to the skillet and cook for about 7 minutes or until the eggs come together. While the eggs cook, move them to 1 side of the skillet, add the prepped sweet potatoes to the other side and allow them to heat through. Remove from heat.

Layer a few large spoonfuls of sweet potatoes in the middle of tortillas. Top with evenly divided feta cheese and eggs. Add salt and black pepper to taste and drizzle a small amount of honey on top of the filling. Wrap the burritos, sealing both ends, and serve warm.

SUGGESTED BEVERAGE: Bloody Marys. See Mason Jar Bloody Marys.

Wild Strawberry Yogurt Parfait

»–Serves 2–»

Wild Colorado Strawberries may be tiny but they are big on taste. In Colorado, you can find them ripe beginning in mid August. They are actually quite easy to spot, once you know what to look for. If you can't find them simply bring your own fresh or frozen strawberries from home.

1 handful of foraged wild strawberries

1 cup granola

1 large container of cream on top vanilla yogurt

1 tablespoon honey

Thoroughly rinse the strawberries and give them a chance to dry off before using.

In your favorite camping cup, layer a handful of your favorite granola in the bottom of the cup. Add two heaping spoonfuls of yogurt on top of the granola.

Drizzle the honey over the yogurt. Add 4 or 5 strawberries and then alternate layers of yogurt and granola until the camping cup is filled.

Add the rest of your strawberries to the top and serve immediately.

SUGGESTED BEVERAGE: Hot coffee. See The Best Camping Coffee In The World.

FORAGING TIPS: Alpine strawberries are very small. As you become aware of what you are looking for you will find that wild strawberries line many trails in Colorado. Look for them in mid August in sunny locations like forest clearings and along roadsides and trails. They can be found between 4,000 and 11,000 feet elevations.

Foraged Porcini Mushroom Egg Scramble

»–Serves 4–»

The Colorado mountains produce some amazing mushrooms. Be cautious that you are sure about the variety, because some can make you quite sick. If you can find them, nothing beats foraged porcini mushrooms. This breakfast is best if you have some time to start a fire in the morning and a chance to heat up the skillet. Serve this dish with bacon, sausage or simply eat it as a main vegetarian breakfast dish.

1 large wild porcini mushroom, sliced
2 tablespoons of unsalted butter
½ teaspoon salt
½ teaspoon freshly ground black pepper
4 eggs

After you find your beautiful wild porcini mushroom, rinse it and store in a cool dry location.

Heat your skillet over the fire and add the butter to let it melt. Once the butter has melted, add the mushroom slices and cook until they begin to brown, about 8 minutes. Add the salt and pepper and cook for 1 minute longer.

When the mushrooms are ready, crack your eggs and

add them directly to the skillet. Stir immediately to break up the yolks and mix thoroughly with the mushrooms.

Cook until the eggs have just become firm, about 5 minutes, and serve warm.

SUGGESTED BEVERAGE: Hot coffee. See The Best Camping Coffee In The World.

FORAGING TIPS: The rule with mushroom foraging is, if you don't know what it is or are not sure, don't eat it. Make sure you take care when selecting mushrooms. Porcini mushrooms, which are my personal favorite, can be found June through August in Colorado. Porcini mushrooms are normally a brown or reddish brown color and found at higher elevations, typically around 10,000 feet. The stem is thick and the cap can sometimes be sticky.

Smoked Colorado Foil Breakfast

»–Serves 2–»

A hearty breakfast with all the fixin's tastes even better outdoors. This dish couldn't be easier to prepare and the smoked paprika, one of my favorite spices, takes it over the edge. If you prefer regular hash browns they can easily be substituted for the sweet potatoes.

1 package frozen sweet potato hash browns

4 eggs

2 elk sausage links

2 teaspoons smoked paprika

salt and freshly ground black pepper to taste

Get your campfire going so you have some nice hot coals to cook with.

Dividing between 2 large pieces of tinfoil evenly split the package of hash browns in 2, forming the base layers of your foil cooking pouch.

Crack 2 fresh eggs on top of each mound of hash browns, then lay a sausage link on the side of the potatoes. Sprinkle a teaspoon of paprika evenly over the top of the mound, followed by salt and pepper to taste.

Carefully close the tinfoil around the ingredients, forming an enclosed, tightly sealed pouch.

Lay the foil pouch on hot coals in the fire, allowing it to cook for 15 minutes. Rotate several times while cooking and serve hot.

SUGGESTED BEVERAGE: Bloody Marys. See Mason Jar Bloody Marys.

Chewy Cherry Breakfast Rounds

»–Serves 4 –»

Sometimes when you roll out of your sleeping bag, the last thing you want to do is start a fire and cook. Make these mountain ready granola bars at home before you go camping and you will be sure to have a delicious and easy breakfast that beats any store bought granola bars. Bonus if you have a food dehydrator and can dry your own Colorado cherries. Cherries will be ripe and available everywhere in Colorado beginning in mid July.

1 cup dried cherries

1 ½ cup rolled oats

¼ cup wheat germ

¼ cup pumpkin seeds

¼ cup walnuts, chopped

¼ cup almonds, chopped

2 tablespoons sesame seeds

2 tablespoons unsalted butter

½ cup maple syrup

2 teaspoons vanilla extract

2 egg whites, lightly beaten

At Home: Preheat the oven to 240 degrees. Combine the cherries, oats, wheat germ, pumpkin seeds, walnuts, almonds and sesame seeds in a large bowl.

In a small saucepan melt the butter with half the maple syrup, stirring well to combine. Remove from heat and stir in the vanilla extract. Pour the butter mixture over the oat mixture and stir well to coat.

Spread the oat mixture evenly into a single layer on a baking sheet. Bake for about 1 ½ hours, stirring every half hour, until the oats are golden brown.

Remove from the oven and transfer the granola to a large bowl. Stir in the remaining maple syrup and egg whites. Coat muffin tin cups with butter or nonstick spray. Press a little less than ½ cup of the oat mixture in each muffin tin and bake for about 40 minutes or until set. Remove from heat and let the granola rounds cool on a wire rack for 20 minutes before removing from the tin.

Store the rounds in a cool area in a sealed container ready for camp.

SUGGESTED BEVERAGE: Hot coffee. See The Best Camping Coffee In The World.

Apple Butter Flapjacks

Serves 4→

I love flapjacks in the morning while camping. The morning chill in the mountains of Colorado begs for a hot breakfast and this recipe satisfies and warms you up from the inside.

DRY INGREDIENTS
1 cup whole wheat flour
¼ cup chopped walnuts
1 teaspoon cinnamon
½ teaspoon salt
½ teaspoon baking powder
½ teaspoon baking soda

WET INGREDIENTS
½ cup buttermilk
½ cup apple butter
1 egg lightly beaten
2 tablespoons canola oil

ON THE SIDE
maple syrup or honey
butter
sliced apples

At Home: Mix the dry ingredients in a large plastic baggie and pack. Mix the wet ingredients in a large mason jar and pack in a cooler.

At Camp: Heat a large skillet over hot coals or a portable gas stove. Mix the wet and dry ingredients well in the plastic baggie. Add butter to the skillet and allow it to melt and coat the bottom completely.

Cut a medium sized hole in the corner of the plastic baggie and squeeze the batter into small circles on the hot skillet, about ½ cup at a time.

Cook for about 3 minutes, or until small bubbles make their way to the top of the batter. Flip and cook for 3 minutes more, or until golden brown.

Serve hot with butter, sliced apples and maple syrup or honey.

SUGGESTED BEVERAGE: Campfire Chai. See Campfire Chai.

Wild Chokecherry Jelly And Biscuits

Serves 4

As a kid my mom and I would always stop when we spotted the abundant and ripe chokecherries that line many dirt roads in Colorado. When made into jam, the sweet taste always reminds me of the mountains. It tastes great on many breakfast items, especially on these campfire biscuits.

FOR THE JELLY

3 ½ pounds foraged chokecherries

8 cups water

1 package pectin

1 ½ cups honey

¼ cup lemon juice

canning jars

FOR THE BISQUITS

2 cups all-purpose flour, plus handful for dusting

1 tablespoon baking powder

1 teaspoon sugar

1 teaspoon salt

8 tablespoons unsalted butter, sliced

1 teaspoon finely grated lemon zest

¾ cup milk, plus more for brushing

At Home: Remove the stems and wash your chokecherries well. Add the chokecherries to a large pot and cover with water. Bring to a boil, then lower the heat to simmer for 15 minutes. Remove from heat and let cool. Using a potato masher, crush the berries to release the juices. Strain through a cheesecloth lined strainer or an old pillow case into a bowl. Let it drain for 3 or 4 hours to ensure all of the juice has been collected.

Add 3 ½ cups of the juice to a large pot, add the pectin and stir well. Bring to a boil, add the honey and lemon juice, stir and bring to a rolling boil. Boil for 2 minutes then remove from heat. Pour the mixture evenly into canning jars and can according to label directions (see canning tips).

Prepare biscuit dough. Whisk the flour, baking powder, sugar, and salt in a bowl. Use your fingers to rub in the butter. It should form little pea sized balls when mixed well. Stir lemon zest into the milk and stir into the flour mixture forming dough. Turn the dough onto a lightly floured surface and roll out to ½ inch thick. Using a biscuit cutter, cut biscuits from the dough and store in tupperware in your camping cooler.

At Camp: Coat a large dutch oven with cooking spray or butter then heat over hot coals. Add pre-cut biscuits to the pan side by side. Cook for 2 minutes, then move the skillet to a slightly cooler part of the fire or area of the grill, cover and let cook for 20 minutes. Flip the biscuit block and cook for 10 minutes longer. Serve with butter and chokecherry jelly.
SUGGESTED BEVERAGE: Hot coffee. See The Best Camping Coffee In The World.

FORAGING TIPS: Eating chokecherries straight from the bush is not recommended. All parts of the chokecherry bush, apart from the berry, contain the poison hydrocyanic acid so don't eat anything but the fruit. For the same reason, be careful not to crush the seeds when extracting the juice from the chokecherries. By drying or cooking the chokecherry you ensure all poisonous residue is destroyed. You can find chokecherry bushes along roads, ditches and creeks all over Colorado. The chokecherries will be ripe and ready for harvesting in August.

CANNING TIPS: When canning jelly, select a large enough kettle for the job. Try to keep the water level well below half to avoid spillover of boiling water. Follow the canning instructions that come with your jars exactly. Always use sterilized canning jars with 2 piece lids. Prepare the jars before canning and keep them warm while preparing your jelly. Fill your jars with jelly mixture to ¼ inch from the top. Be sure to process the sealed jars that contain the jelly in a bath of boiling water for at least 10 minutes to prevent the growth of mold and to properly seal.

Wild Colorado Chokecherries

Pigs In A Morning Blanket

⸫Serves 4→
I first tasted this dish in Germany but quickly adapted it to my camping adventures. If you are hungry, or have a long day of hiking ahead of you, this dish will hold you over until lunch time without a problem.

1 cup whole-wheat flour
1 tablespoon sugar
2 teaspoons baking powder
1 teaspoon salt
1 egg, beaten
1 cup milk
2 tablespoons olive oil
2 tablespoons unsalted butter
4 large breakfast link pork sausages
maple syrup

In a large plastic baggie combine the flour, sugar, baking powder, salt, egg, milk and oil, seal, and mix well by squeezing the ingredients inside the bag with your hand.

Over a portable gas stove, or campfire, heat a skillet and add the butter to melt.

Cut one corner of the plastic baggie and squeeze the

mixture into the skillet, making the pancakes as large as you like. You will be wrapping the sausages with the pancakes so make them big enough for this purpose.

Cook for 5 minutes on each side until golden brown. Set aside and cover with a cloth to keep warm.

Add the sausages to the hot skillet and cook for about 10 minutes, turning several times until golden brown. Remove from heat.

Place 1 sausage in the middle of each pancake, drizzle with maple syrup, wrap completely and serve.

SUGGESTED BEVERAGE: Hot coffee. See The Best Camping Coffee In The World.

Denver Omelette

Serves 2 →

Found on most breakfast menus in Colorado, this classic dish is easy to cook and somehow tastes even better when dining outside. I like to use extra sharp raw cheddar cheese which makes the omelette taste better than those you find in most restaurants.

1 tablespoon butter
¼ cup yellow onion, diced
½ cup green bell pepper, diced
¼ cup ham, cubed
4 eggs
¼ cup sharp cheddar cheese, shredded
salt and freshly ground black pepper to taste
hot sauce

Heat a large skillet over hot coals or on a portable gas stove. Add butter to the pan and sauté the onion, bell pepper and ham for 4 minutes.

While the onion mixture cooks, whisk the eggs in a large bowl. Remove the onion mixture from the fire and add to the bowl, mixing with the eggs. Add the cheddar cheese to the egg mixture. Add more butter to the pan if needed.

Pour the egg mixture into the pan, cover and let cook for 4 or 5 minutes, or until the edges begin to firm. Using a spatula, fold the omelette in half and cook for 3 minutes. Flip to the other side and cook for 3 minutes more, or until the middle is cooked through and the cheese has melted.

Remove from heat, sprinkle with salt and pepper and serve with your favorite hot sauce.

SUGGESTED BEVERAGE: Bloody Marys. See Mason Jar Bloody Marys.

Pepper Bacon & Egg Breakfast Sandwiches

⏲Serves 2→

If you like breakfast sandwiches then you will love these hot and delicious, almost grilled cheese like, morning treats.

2 slices of pepper bacon

4 eggs

4 slices of whole wheat bread

4 thin slices of sharp cheddar cheese

1 teaspoon mayo

1 teaspoon sriracha sauce

Heat a large skillet over hot coals or on a portable gas stove. Add bacon to the pan and cook until crispy, flipping a few times, about 10 minutes.

Remove the bacon from the pan and place on a paper towel. Leave the bacon drippings in the pan and add the eggs, stirring well to scramble and cook for about 5 minutes. Remove the eggs from the pan and divide evenly onto 2 slices of bread. Top the eggs with evenly divided cheese.

Spread mayo and sriracha sauce evenly on the other 2 slices of bread and place on top of the sandwich. Place both sandwiches in the skillet and cook for about 3 minutes on each side, or until the bread is golden brown and the cheese has melted.

Serve immediately.

SUGGESTED BEVERAGE: Bloody Marys. See Mason Jar Bloody Marys.

Maple Cream Cheese French Toast

Serves 4

French toast is incredibly easy to make, which makes it a great camping breakfast item. I like to serve this dish with a side of crispy maple bacon.

1 egg

½ cup whole milk

2 tablespoons sugar

2 teaspoons cinnamon

½ teaspoon vanilla extract

1 cup maple cream cheese

8 thick cut slices of french bread

2 tablespoons butter

¼ cup maple syrup

4 slices of maple bacon, cooked

Preheat a cast iron skillet over hot coals or a camp stove.

Whisk the egg, milk, sugar, cinnamon and the vanilla together in a bowl.

Spread cream cheese over 4 slices of bread and top with remaining slices. Add the butter to the pan and swirl to coat.

Dip the sandwiches in the egg mixture, then cook, turning once, until brown and crisp. This should take about 6 minutes total.

Serve the French toast warm with maple syrup and bacon.

SUGGESTED BEVERAGE: Hot coffee. See The Best Camping Coffee In The World.

Breakfast Bagels With Cilantro Sauce

⏲Serves 2→

Sauce has the ability to elevate any dish from OK to amazing. If you love garlic, cilantro and sauce then this breakfast sandwich will quickly become a go to for your camping trips. While experimenting with sauces for dinner, I decided to try this tangy sauce in the morning on a bagel, with eggs and now eat this dish all the time.

1 ¾ cups cilantro leaves

¼ cup white onion, diced

1 cup olive oil

2 tablespoons rice wine vinegar

1 teaspoon salt

1 teaspoon ground cumin

1 teaspoon ground coriander

½ teaspoon ground black pepper

2 garlic cloves

2 jalapeño peppers, seeded

2 eggs

2 everything bagels

4 slices cheddar cheese

At Home: In a blender, combine the cilantro, onion, olive oil, vinegar, salt, cumin, coriander, pepper, garlic and jalapeño. Blend until smooth and store in mason jar. Pack in a cooler for camp.

At Camp: Heat a skillet over hot coals or on a portable gas stove. Add some olive oil or butter to the skillet, swirling to coat. Add the eggs and cook until over easy, about 5 minutes or until the clear egg white becomes a solid white color. We want the yolk in the center to remain runny.

Slice the bagels in half and on the bottom half of each bagel layer cheese, then an egg. Spread a generous amount of the cilantro sauce on the top half of the bagel. Place the top half on the egg half, to form a bagel sandwich.

Serve immediately.

SUGGESTED BEVERAGE: Hot coffee. See The Best Camping Coffee In The World.

Colorado Honey Almond Granola

Serves 2 →

My go to dish when I want a quick no fuss breakfast while camping is granola and some yogurt. Making your granola at home is both economical and incredibly delicious. Make this granola at home ahead of time and you can even double it to make it last for a few camping trips. Using local Colorado honey makes it all that much better.

1 teaspoon coconut oil
¼ cup local Colorado honey
2 tablespoons unsalted butter, melted
½ teaspoon vanilla extract
1 ½ cups uncooked rolled oats
½ cup whole wheat flour
½ cup raw almonds, chopped
¼ teaspoon pink Himalayan salt
½ teaspoon cinnamon
¼ teaspoon cardamom

At Home: Preheat the oven to 350 degrees and grease a baking sheet with the coconut oil.

In a small bowl, combine the honey, butter and vanilla. In a separate bowl combine the rolled oats, flour, almonds, salt, cinnamon and cardamom.

Add the honey mixture to the oat mixture and stir until combined.

Spread the mix into a single layer on the greased baking sheet and bake for 12 minutes.

Toss the granola and bake for 6 minutes more.

Let cool and store in ball jars or plastic bags and take with you camping. Serve with plain or vanilla yogurt.

SUGGESTED BEVERAGE: Campfire Chai. See Campfire Chai.

COLORADO HONEY: Colorado honey bees produce some high quality delicious honey. I prefer pure raw and unfiltered Colorado honey. Rumor has it that eating local honey can even help with allergies. The bees in Colorado feed on local wildflowers and nectars which offer a unique flavor profile you can find nowhere else.

Dutch Oven Honey Monkey Bread

🍽Serves 4→

Monkey bread is a tradition in my family that is typically served in the morning during holiday family get togethers like Thanksgiving. This recipe is adapted for your next trip to the mountains, for a new camping tradition.

1 stick unsalted butter

½ cup brown sugar

¼ teaspoon salt

¼ cup honey

2 tablespoons cinnamon

½ cup white sugar

18 count frozen dinner rolls, thawed

Heat a large dutch oven over hot coals. Add ½ stick of butter, brown sugar and salt and cook until the butter has melted and the sugar has dissolved. Add the honey and simmer 6 minutes, or until the syrup has thickened.

In another small pan, melt the remaining ½ stick of butter. In a shallow bowl, combine the cinnamon and white sugar. Divide each dinner roll in half and using your hands roll each into a ball. Dip the ball in the melted butter, then roll the ball in the cinnamon mixture until well coated.

Place each coated ball of dough into the large skillet with the honey syrup. Add the top to the dutch oven, return to coals and cover the top of the dutch oven completely with hot coals. Allow it to cook for 30 minutes and check to see if the rolls are firm to touch. If they are not done return them to the coals and cook for a few minutes longer.

Remove from heat and allow them to rest, uncovered for a few minutes before serving.

SUGGESTED BEVERAGE: Hot coffee. See The Best Camping Coffee In The World.

Hearty Mountain Breakfast

⯈Serves 2→

If you are planning to scale a mountain then this breakfast will start you off right. It combines all breakfast favorites into 1 satisfying dutch oven. I like local elk sausage in this recipe but you can easily substitute pork if you prefer.

4 strips of pepper bacon

1 lb elk sausage or pork

1 yellow onion, chopped

3 garlic cloves, minced

1 green bell pepper, chopped

1 red bell pepper, chopped

1 large package frozen hash browns

12 eggs, beaten

1 package shredded Mexican cheese blend

hot sauce

Cook the bacon in a large dutch oven over hot coals for about 10 minutes, flipping half way through. You want the bacon brown and crispy. Remove the bacon and place on a paper towel. When cool, crumble the bacon.

Add the sausage, onion and garlic to the dutch oven and cook for about 10 minutes, stirring often to break up the sausage and ensure it is evenly cooked.

Add the bell peppers and hash browns and mix everything together well. Cook for about 18 minutes or until the hash browns are hot.

Pour the eggs over the top of the mixture, cover the top of the dutch oven completely with hot coals. Allow it to bake for about 45 minutes, and if needed replace the coals on top of the dutch oven with fresh hot coals to keep it cooking properly. The eggs should be firm when done.

Remove from heat, sprinkle the cheese and crumbled bacon on top, cover again and allow it to sit for 5 minutes, then serve with hot sauce when the cheese has melted.

SUGGESTED BEVERAGE: Bloody Marys. See Mason Jar Bloody Marys.

Cardamom Spiced Oatmeal

Serves 2

This breakfast is perfect for cold mornings when you wake up to unexpected snow or frost. Cardamom is a sweet and unique spice that I love in my oatmeal and it is perfect in this hot breakfast.

2 cups water
1 cup quick cooking rolled oats
1 teaspoon ground cardamom
1 teaspoon cinnamon
¼ cup sliced almonds
1 tablespoon unsalted butter
1 tablespoon maple syrup

Boil the water in a pot over a fire or in a Jetboil. Remove the water from heat and add the oats, cardamom and cinnamon. Stir the ingredients together well and let it sit for a few minutes until the oats have absorbed the water.

Divide the oatmeal evenly between 2 bowls, then top evenly with sliced almonds, butter and maple syrup.

Serve immediately.

SUGGESTED BEVERAGE: Campfire Chai. See Campfire Chai.

Colorado Stout Pancakes

⏲Serves 4→

Beer and pancakes may not seem like a likely combination but the flavors packed in dark stout beers are perfect for breakfast. This recipe features Hammer & Sickle, Russian Imperial Stout from Renegade Brewing Company in Denver, but you can use any stout style beer from you favorite Colorado brewer.

Pancake mix
1 can Hammer & Sickle, Russian Imperial Stout beer
¼ cup chopped walnuts
2 tablespoons butter, plus more for serving
maple syrup

Follow the package directions of the pancake mix and

instead of adding water, add beer. Add the walnuts and stir to combine well. Let the mixture stand for a few minutes.

Heat the butter in a large cast iron skillet over hot coals or on a portable gas stove and swirl to coat the pan. Spoon the pancake mix into the pan in your desired pancake size, and cook for 3 to 4 minutes on both sides, or until golden brown.

Serve with maple syrup and butter.

SUGGESTED BEVERAGE: Hammer & Sickle, Russian Imperial Stout - Renegade Brewing Company (Denver, Colorado)

Green Chile Breakfast Burritos

Serves 4

Perhaps my favorite camping breakfast of all is a hearty breakfast burrito stuffed with all types of things. I eat a lot of green chiles while camping and normally have some leftover. Stuffed inside a tortilla with cheese and a bevy of other ingredients these burritos are sure to satisfy hungry campers.

4 strips of applewood smoked bacon
1 26 oz package of frozen hash browns
6 eggs, beaten
1 white onion, diced
1 green bell pepper, diced
2 cups cheddar cheese, shredded
3 roasted green chile peppers
4 large tortillas, warmed by the fire
salt and pepper to taste

Heat a large cast iron skillet over hot coals or a portable gas stove. Add the bacon and cook for about 5 minutes on each side. When crispy, remove from heat and place on a paper towel. Crumble the bacon when it has cooled.

Add the hash browns to the bacon grease and cook

until browned, about 8 minutes. Make sure to flip the hash browns a few times for even browning.

When the hash browns are done, add the onion, bell pepper, crumbled bacon and eggs to the pan. Cook until the eggs are set, about 6 minutes, stirring as needed.

Add the cheese and stir to combine. Lay the green chile peppers on top of the mixture and cook until the cheese has melted and the eggs are completely cooked.

Evenly divide the filling between 4 tortillas, wrap and serve warm.

SUGGESTED BEVERAGE: Bloody Marys. See Mason Jar Bloody Marys.

Kale And Goat Cheese Cups

⮕Serves 4→

Chock full of eggs, kale and cheese this breakfast is your soon to be camping staple. You will need a drop biscuit pan for this recipe, or if you don't have one, just cook it all together in a skillet, then slice it up after it is done.

3 tablespoons olive oil
2 garlic cloves, sliced
1 bunch kale, chopped
¼ teaspoon crushed red pepper
6 large eggs
salt to taste
freshly ground black pepper to taste
½ teaspoon thyme
¼ cup goat cheese, crumbled

Heat a small skillet over a campfire or on a portable gas stove and add the olive oil, swirling to coat the pan. Add the garlic and cook for 30 seconds. Add the kale and red pepper and cook until the kale has wilted, about 4 minutes.

In a large bowl, whisk the eggs together with the salt and pepper. Add the cooked kale and thyme to the egg mixture, stirring to combine.

Grease the drop biscuit pan with leftover olive oil and add the egg mixture to the individual cups in the drop biscuit pan. Evenly sprinkle the goat cheese on top of each filled cup.

Cook over hot coals or a portable gas stove, covered with tinfoil, for about 15 minutes.

Remove from heat and serve hot.

SUGGESTED BEVERAGE: Hot coffee. See The Best Camping Coffee In The World.

Apple Cinnamon Granola

🍽Serves 4→

Make a big batch of this granola at home before your camping trip and it should last all weekend. I like this recipe with plain yogurt and Colorado honey drizzled on top.

4 cups old-fashioned rolled oats

1 ½ cups walnuts, chopped

¼ cup brown sugar

½ teaspoon salt

¾ teaspoon ground cinnamon

¼ cup olive oil

¼ cup honey plus more for drizzling

1 teaspoon vanilla extract

1 ½ cups dried apples

3 cups plain yogurt

At Home: Preheat oven to 300 degrees. Mix the oats, walnuts, sugar, salt and cinnamon together in a large bowl.

In a small saucepan heat the oil and honey until combined, about 2 minutes. Add the vanilla to the saucepan and whisk. Remove from heat.

Pour the liquid over the oat mixture and stir gently with a wooden spoon. Spread the granola on a cookie sheet and bake for 45 minutes. Stir the mixture every 15 minutes to ensure the oats don't burn.

Transfer the granola to a cooling rack and allow to cool completely. Stir in the dried apples and store in a large plastic baggie at room temperature. Pack for camp.

At Camp: Serve the granola with yogurt and drizzle honey on top.

SUGGESTED BEVERAGE: Hot coffee. See The Best Camping Coffee In The World.

Sweet Potato Pancakes

Serves 4→

I eat a lot of sweet potatoes and these pancakes allow me to do so for breakfast. Sweet potatoes are especially satisfying for a lazy summer camping breakfast. These pancakes are complex and filling.

1 small sweet potato

1 cup whole wheat flour

2 teaspoons baking powder

1 teaspoon cinnamon

½ teaspoon nutmeg

¼ teaspoon cardamon

¼ teaspoon salt

1 egg

1 ¼ cup whole milk

1 teaspoon maple syrup, plus more for serving

1 tablespoon unsalted butter, softened, plus more for frying and serving

½ teaspoon vanilla extract

At Home: Bake the sweet potato for 45 minutes at 350 degrees. Or you can microwave 8 minutes until tender. When the sweet potato cools, mash it well and store it in tupperware in a camping cooler.

Combine the wheat flour, baking powder, cinnamon, nutmeg, cardamon and salt in a large plastic baggie, seal and shake well. Pack for camp.

At Camp: In a large bowl combine the egg, mashed sweet potato, milk, maple syrup, butter and vanilla. Mix well, then add the dry ingredients you stored in the plastic baggie to the bowl.

Mix all of the ingredients together well. The mixture should be runny. If it is too dry, add some extra milk.

Heat extra butter in a large cast iron skillet over hot coals or a portable gas stove.

Pour about ½ cup of batter for each pancake, in the hot skillet. Cook until the edges of the pancake start to firm and bubbles come to the top in the middle, about 4 minutes. Flip and cook for about 4 minutes more. Remove the pancakes from the skillet and repeat with the remaining batter.

Serve warm topped with butter and maple syrup.

SUGGESTED BEVERAGE: Hot coffee. See The Best Camping Coffee In The World.

Brown Sugar Grilled Grapefruit

Serves 4

This common breakfast item gets a foodie facelift in this flavor packed, easy breakfast recipe.

4 grapefruits, sliced in half
1 tablespoon cinnamon
1 tablespoon brown sugar

At Home: Combine the cinnamon and brown sugar in a small plastic baggie and pack for camp.

At Camp: Grill the grapefruit, cut sides down, over a campfire for about 10 minutes. Flip, sprinkle the cinnamon and sugar mixture over the top and grill peel side down for about 5 minutes longer.

Serve warm.

SUGGESTED BEVERAGE: Hot coffee. See The Best Camping Coffee In The World.

Cheesy Jalapeño Scrambled Eggs

Serves 4

This simple scrambled egg dish will start your day off with a kick. I like to eat this dish with toasted whole wheat english muffins on the side.

3 tablespoons unsalted butter
1 jalapeño, seeded and sliced
1 small yellow onion, finely diced
10 large eggs, lightly beaten
¼ cup whole milk
salt and freshly ground black pepper to taste
4 oz Colorado goat cheese
2 tablespoons chives, chopped

Heat a large cast iron skillet over hot coals or a portable gas stove. Add the butter, melt and add the jalapeño and onion. Sauté for 5 minutes or until the onion is translucent.

Meanwhile combine the eggs, milk, salt and pepper in a large bowl. Add the egg mixture to the skillet and stir well to combine. Cook until the eggs come together and are cooked through, about 5 minutes.

Stir in the goat cheese, remove from heat and serve

warm topped with fresh chives.

SUGGESTED BEVERAGE: Spicy Bloody Marys. See Mason Jar Bloody Marys.

Breakfast Quinoa Bowls

⁃Serves 4→

Quinoa for breakfast? Absolutely. This breakfast dish is as delicious as it is healthy. It even packs enough fuel to climb a 14er.

1 cup multicolored quinoa, rinsed

1 ½ cups water

½ cup orange juice

1 tablespoon olive oil

½ cup slivered almonds

½ cup dried apricots, cut into quarters

2 tablespoons maple syrup

¼ teaspoon grated orange zest

½ teaspoon cinnamon

¼ cup ricotta cheese

At Home: Cook the quinoa with the water and orange juice, covered, in a small saucepan for 15 minutes, or until the liquid has been absorbed. Remove from heat. When cool store in tupperware in a camping cooler.

At Camp: Heat the olive oil in a cast iron skillet over hot coals or a portable gas stove. Add the almonds and cook for about 4 minutes. Add the apricots, maple syrup, orange zest and cinnamon. Cook for about 1 minute, or until heated through.

Add the quinoa to the skillet and stir until well combined and hot. Serve warm in bowls, topped with a big spoonful of ricotta cheese.

SUGGESTED BEVERAGE: Campfire Chai. See Campfire Chai.

After a day of exploring the Colorado outdoors, food somehow just tastes better. When local ingredients, foraged or farmed, are added to camping meals there is nothing like it. I like food cooked over an open fire for the best flavor and enjoy slow roasting my ingredients to perfection.

I enjoy eating local and tend to cook what is in season and available. Whether that means trout which I catch myself, foraged wild chives, garden grown tomatoes or Colorado elk, the proof is in the flavor. Foraging takes effort but it can also be fun to keep an eye out for edible wild mushrooms as you explore the great outdoors. Foraging is the ultimate treasure hunt, so I suggest giving it a try before substituting store bought ingredients. I have provided helpful tips on how to find the wild ingredients suggested.

As with breakfast, I like to prep some of my ingredients before getting to camp to save time and dishes. I don't like bringing a cutting board with me to the woods so I tend to chop everything at home and simply store them in a cooler.

You will need some basic cooking equipment to prepare the dinner recipes listed. These include:

- Large Mixing Bowl
- Sharp Knife
- Tinfoil
- Portable Gas Stove (if you prefer not to cook over a fire)
- Dutch Oven / Large Cast Iron Skillet
- Portable Metal Grill Rack
- Jetboil (option to boil water)

- Paella Pan

A good dinner goes great with a good drink and luckily, here in Colorado, we have a plethora of craft beers and locally produced drinks to choose from. I have paired the dishes listed with my suggested beverage of choice. These are meant to be a guide to get the most flavor from your meal.

Green Chile Skillet Tots

⸙Serves 4→

This dish is the perfect way to end a day of adventuring outdoors. Nothing beats the spicy kick of green chile and this gooey, one skillet dish is easy and delicious.

4 tablespoons unsalted butter

1 package frozen tater tots

1 jar green chile

1 ½ cups shredded cheddar cheese

Give your fire a chance to form some very hot coals before beginning this dish. Heat a large cast iron skillet over the hot coals.

Add the butter to the skillet and allow it to melt completely. Swirl the butter to evenly coat the bottom of the skillet.

Add the tater tots and cook for 5 minutes, stir, then cook for 5 minutes more or until they start to brown and become crispy.

Evenly pour the entire jar of green chile over the top of the tots, and smooth with a spoon. Cover the green chile evenly with the cheese.

Cover and cook for 5 minutes until the green chile

begins to bubble and the cheese has melted. Serve warm.

SUGGESTED BEVERAGE: Rye IPA - Odell Brewing Company (Ft. Collins, Colorado)

Campfire Quesadillas

⟶Serves 2⟶

This dish requires some prep work before you leave for your camping trip. You haven't lived until you have tried these smokey quesadillas, finished over an open flame. I almost always include this dish in my weekend camping plans.

2 tablespoons olive oil

salt and freshly ground black pepper to taste

1 skinless boneless chicken breast

½ cup red bell pepper, diced

½ cup green bell pepper, diced

½ cup white onion, diced

1 garlic clove, minced

2 cups shredded cheddar cheese or pepper jack

4 large flour tortillas

At Home: Heat a sauté pan over medium heat. Add a tablespoon of the olive oil and swirl to coat the pan.

Sprinkle salt and pepper on both sides of the chicken breast. Add the chicken to the pan cooking until lightly brown on the bottom, about 5 minutes. Flip the chicken and cook for an additional 5 minutes, or until fully cooked and white all the way through. Remove from the pan and let the chicken rest for 10 minutes before cutting.

Meanwhile, add another tablespoon of olive oil to the pan. Add the red bell pepper, green bell pepper and onion to the pan. Sauté the vegetables for 5 minutes. Add the garlic and cook for 1 minute more. Remove from heat, add salt and pepper and mix well.

Slice the chicken breast into thin strips and add them to a large plastic baggie. Add the vegetable mixture to the plastic baggie, seal and shake to combine the mixture well. Store in a cooler for camp.

At Camp: Working on a flat surface, layer a handful of cheese, then some chicken mixture, finishing with another handful of cheese, on a tortilla. Top with another tortilla to form your uncooked quesadilla. Repeat.

Over a fire, level a portable metal grill rack over hot coals. Place the quesadillas on top of the grill and cook for 5 minutes, watching closely so it does not burn. Flip and cook for 5 minutes, or until the tortilla is crispy and brown.

SUGGESTED BEVERAGE: Mexican Logger - Ska Brewing Company (Durango, Colorado)

Hatch Green Chile Grilled Cheese

Serves 4

Green chiles are served and roasted roadside all over Colorado during the hot summer months. Pick some up and enjoy this delicious, hot and cheesy sandwich while camping.

3 roasted hatch green chiles, sliced lengthwise into thin strips
¼ teaspoon salt
¾ cup sharp cheddar cheese, shredded
¼ cup mozzarella cheese, shredded
8 slices whole wheat bread
1 tablespoon unsalted butter

Place the green chiles in a bowl, add salt, then toss. Sprinkle half mozzarella and half cheddar evenly on 4 slices of bread.

Layer evenly divided chiles on the cheese, then top with remaining cheese and remaining bread slices.

Heat a large cast iron skillet over your campfire or a portable gas stove. Add the butter to the pan and swirl to evenly coat. Cook each sandwich 4 minutes on each side, until the bread is golden brown and the cheese has melted.

Serve immediately.

SUGGESTED BEVERAGE: Green Chile Lager - Tommyknocker Brewery (Idaho Springs, Colorado)

Hobo Packets With Foraged Wild Onions

⏵Serves 4→

Hobo packets are easy, filling and delicious cooked over campfire coals. You can easily enjoy this recipe if you can't find any wild onions, but if you can, the onions will make this dish special.

2 skinless, boneless chicken breasts, cubed
5 button mushrooms, sliced
1 red bell pepper, seeded and sliced into strips
3 garlic cloves, minced
10 fingerling potatoes, halved
1 lemon, juiced
¼ cup olive oil
¼ cup foraged wild onions, chopped
salt and freshly ground black pepper to taste

In a large plastic baggie combine the chicken, mushrooms, bell pepper, garlic and potatoes. Pour in the lemon juice and olive oil. Shake the bag until the ingredients are well combined.

Divide the mixture evenly on 4 sheets of aluminum foil. Wrap the aluminum foil around the mix, securing at the top to form 4 sealed packets.

Cook the packets over hot coals in a campfire until the chicken has cooked through and the potatoes are tender, about 45 minutes. Open the packets and top with wild onions. Add salt and pepper to taste.

Serve immediately.

SUGGESTED BEVERAGE: Iced Tea - See Wild Mint Sun Tea.

FORAGING TIPS: Wild onions can be found in early spring and are abundant until late fall. They have wide flat green leaves and are most easily identifiable by a strong onion smell. They look similar to a poisonous plant called death camas so use caution. When bloomed the onion has pink flowers and death camas have white flowers which makes it easy to tell them apart. You can find wild onions all over Colorado, especially in moist meadows and on hillsides.

Buffalo Chicken Tinfoil Baked Potatoes

Serves 2 →

These easy, tinfoil packets of goodness, are absolutely loaded with flavor. If you like buffalo sauce then you will love this recipe.

1 skinless, boneless chicken breast
salt and freshly ground black pepper to taste
¼ cup sour cream
1 tablespoon celery leaves, chopped
¼ cup hot wing sauce
2 large potatoes
¼ cup blue cheese crumbles
4 celery sticks, cut into 2 inch pieces
4 carrots, cut into 2 inch pieces

At Home: Cook your chicken breast either on the grill or in a sauté pan before you leave. Make sure to sprinkle with salt and pepper before cooking. When cool, chop the chicken into cubes and store in a large plastic baggie. Add salt, pepper, sour cream, celery leaves and hot wing sauce to the baggie, seal, and shake to combine the ingredients. Pack in a cooler for camp.

At Camp: Sprinkle the potatoes with salt and pepper

and enclose completely in large sheets of tinfoil. Place the packages on hot coals in the campfire and cook for 45 minutes to an hour, rotating at least once.

Remove the potatoes from the coals, let cool for 5 minutes, then open. Cut the potato in half lengthwise, and using a fork, shred the potato. Evenly divide the chicken mixture on top of each potato and combine with your fork so the hot potato warms the chicken mixture. Top with blue cheese crumbles and serve with the celery sticks and carrots.

SUGGESTED BEVERAGE: Joe's Premium American Pilsner - Avery Brewing Company (Boulder, Colorado)

Colorado Elk Sausage Campfire Pizza

⏲Serves 4→

Grilled campfire pizza, oh my! This dish makes an appearance on my camping menu every summer and features local elk, which is available all over Colorado.

1 lb ground Italian style elk sausage
1 fennel bulb, thinly sliced
½ cup yellow onion, thinly sliced
¼ cup olive oil
salt and freshly ground black pepper to taste
½ tablespoon dried oregano
½ cup shredded fontina cheese
store bought pizza dough

Prepare your campfire long before you plan to cook. You will need a nice bed of hot coals to properly cook your pizza.

Heat a large cast iron skillet over the campfire and add the sausage to the skillet. Cook the sausage until browned, about 8 minutes. Remove the sausage and set aside.

Add the fennel and onion to the skillet and cook in the sausage fat for 5 minutes or until tender. Add olive oil, salt, pepper and oregano, stirring well and remove the skillet from the fire.

Roll out the dough on a clean flat surface using a water bottle as your pizza roller. Cook the flattened dough on a portable metal grill rack over the fire for 3 minutes, then flip and repeat on the other side until crisp. Remove the crust from the grill and top with the sausage and fennel mixture, spreading evenly. Top with the fontina cheese.

Return the pizza to the grill, placing a large metal bowl or tinfoil over the top of the pizza to trap the heat, which will help melt the cheese. Cook for 3 minutes, or until the cheese has melted.

Slice and serve hot.

SUGGESTED BEVERAGE: Colorado Syrah - Balistreri Vineyard (Denver, Colorado)

Grammy's Corn Crusted Rainbow Trout

⏲Serves 2→

This simple recipe comes from my grandmother, who I called Grammy. I used to spend my summers fishing near Gunnison, Colorado with my grandfather. We would catch fresh rainbow trout, clean them and bring them back to our mountain cabin where Grammy would work her magic, turning them into a delicious simple meal. If you fish, this is my favorite way to cook the day's catch.

1 cup yellow corn meal
1 teaspoon salt
1 teaspoon freshly ground black pepper
2 fresh caught trout, cleaned
1 cup whole milk
2 tablespoons butter

In a shallow bowl mix the corn meal, salt and pepper. Dip each cleaned trout in milk, then dip them in the corn meal mixture, coating the outside completely with corn meal.

Add the butter to a medium sized skillet and heat over hot coals or on portable camp stove. When the butter has melted add the trout to the hot pan allowing it to cook for 5 minutes on each side, or until brown and crispy.

Serve warm.

SUGGESTED BEVERAGE: Colorado Chardonnay - Plum Creek (Palisade, Colorado)

FISH CLEANING TIPS: Cleaning a fish is the process of removing the guts of the trout and anything you are not going to eat, leaving you with fillets. I like to clean the fish riverside right before I take them back to camp. All you need is a simple pocket knife for the job. First remove the scales by scraping from tail to head several times on each side of the trout with the dull edge of your knife. Next, cut the fish's belly open from the exit hole just above the tail to the head. Spread the belly open and remove the innards with your hand and discard. You should now see the thick vein that lines the backbone of the fish. Firmly run your thumb fingernail from the tail end of the fish to the head, scraping away the blood vein along the backbone. Before cooking, rinse the trout well with clean water inside and out. If you prefer you can cut off the head but I always cook the trout with the head still on because that is the way my grandmother did it.

Bruschetta Baked Potatoes

⏲Serves 2→

In this dish, Italy meets fresh Colorado grown basil, heirloom tomatoes and baked potatoes cooked to perfection in your campfire.

2 large russet potatoes
2 large heirloom tomatoes, diced
2 tablespoons olive oil
2 tablespoons red wine vinegar
½ cup fresh basil, chopped
1 cup mozzarella, diced
salt and pepper to taste

Sprinkle the potatoes with salt and pepper and enclose completely in large sheets of tinfoil. Place the packages on hot coals in the fire and cook for 45 minutes to an hour, rotating at least once.

Meanwhile, combine the tomatoes, olive oil, vinegar and basil in a bowl, mixing well to combine.

Remove the potatoes from the coals, let cool for 5 minutes, then open. Cut the potato in half lengthwise, and using a fork, shred the potato. Top with mozzarella, directly on the hot potato so it can melt and serve with the tomato mixture spooned over the top.

SUGGESTED BEVERAGE: Sangria - See Colorado Peach Sangria.

Foraged Purslane Chickpea Tahini Wraps

🞂Serves 4→

Purslane is packed with vitamins and omega-3 fatty acids. It can be found growing wild in many parts of Colorado. The flavor has a mild hint of lemon and herbs which makes it a great addition to this vegetarian wrap. It is said that purslane was Gandhi's favorite food.

1 tablespoon tahini
1 lemon, juiced
1 tablespoon olive oil
1 tablespoon rice vinegar
1 teaspoon cumin
salt and freshly ground black pepper to taste
1 can chickpeas, drained
4 cups wild purslane leaves
½ cup purslane stems, finely chopped
½ cup green onions, chopped
¼ cup basil leaves, torn
1 garlic clove, minced

5 cherry tomatoes, halved

4 large flour tortillas

At Home: In a large bowl combine the the tahini, lemon juice, olive oil, rice vinegar, cumin, salt and pepper and mix well.

Add the chickpeas and combine. Store the mixture in a plastic baggie or tupperware and pack in a cooler for camp.

At Camp: Once you find your purslane, wash them well and add them, along with the chopped stems to a large bowl. Combine with the green onions, basil leaves, garlic and tomatoes, then add the tahini mixture you prepared at home. Toss to combine.

Evenly divide and spoon the mixture on the tortillas and wrap before serving.

SUGGESTED BEVERAGE: Cocktail - See Colorado Honey Thyme.

FORAGING TIPS: Purslane has plump, glossy leaves, and you may have already spotted It growing in your lawn or even at a farmers market. Purslane can also be found growing near many campsites in Colorado. Look for it in late June. It looks like a succulent that grows close to the ground. The best tasting part of the plant are the rounded leaves. When harvesting be sure to avoid anywhere that has been sprayed with weed killing chemicals.

Hipster Hobo Hash

Serves 2

If you have a garden in Colorado, or like to visit the farmers markets during the summer, this dish leaves room for wonderful creativity. Fill it with any veggies that are in season and enjoy.

1 cup zucchini, diced
1 cup yellow summer squash, diced
1 sweet potato, cut into small cubes
1 cup garden cherry tomatoes
½ cup yellow onion, chopped
1 lemon, juiced
½ cup olive oil
2 tablespoons Italian seasoning
salt and freshly ground black pepper to taste
2 eggs

In a large plastic baggie or bowl combine the zucchini, squash, potato, tomato, yellow onion and seasonings. Pour in the lemon juice and olive oil. Shake the bag or stir until the ingredients are mixed well.

Divide the mixture in half evenly on 2 sheets of tinfoil. Crack 1 egg on the top of each pile. Wrap the tinfoil around the mix, securing at the top to form a sealed packet. Try to leave space on the top to avoid breaking the egg yolk.

Cook on hot coals in the campfire for about 15 minutes. Remove from heat and let cool for 5 minutes. Open the packets and serve immediately.

SUGGESTED BEVERAGE: Bridal Veil Rye Pale Ale - Telluride Brewing Company (Telluride, Colorado)

Giant Pigs In A Blanket On A Stick

Serves 4 →

We have all enjoyed a sausage or hot dog cooked on a stick over an open fire while camping. This is a way to spice up your tradition with a twist on a popular party snack.

4 spicy andouli pork sausages
1 package refrigerated crescent roll dough
ketchup
german mustard

Cook the sausage on a green stick over the fire for 10 minutes, slowly spinning, until fat starts to drip into the fire.

Remove from the fire, let cool and wrap each sausage with 1 sheet of dough. Cook for an additional 10 minutes over the fire, slowly spinning, until the dough is light brown and cooked through.

Serve with ketchup and mustard.

SUGGESTED BEVERAGE: Weissbier - Prost Brewing Company (Denver, Colorado)

Colorado Blue Cheese Buffalo Burgers

🞏Serves 4→

You can find grass-fed, grass-finished buffalo or bison meat producers all over Colorado. These burgers turn out juicy and delicious every time and are extremely satisfying after a long day of hiking.

1 lb ground buffalo
½ cup whole wheat bread crumbs
1 egg
2 tablespoons Worcestershire sauce
1 garlic clove, minced
½ teaspoon freshly ground black pepper
4 tablespoons crumbled blue cheese
4 hamburger buns
cooking spray

In a large bowl mix the buffalo, bread crumbs, egg, Worcestershire sauce, garlic and pepper. Form the mixture into 4 burger patties with your hands.

Heat a portable grill rack over hot coals and coat with cooking spray. Place the patties on the grill and cook for 4 minutes. Flip each patty and top with 1 tablespoon each of blue cheese. Cook for 4 minutes longer for medium-rare, and until the cheese has melted.

Server on buns with your favorite condiments. I like a good grainy german mustard.

SUGGESTED BEVERAGE: Peach Beer - See Honey Palisade Peach Beer.

Hot Dogs With Homemade Chow Chow

Serves 4→

Chow chow is a pickled relish that takes your hot dogs from ho hum to wow. Make a batch of chow chow at home and enjoy it throughout the summer on all of your hot dogs and hamburgers.

20 cups chopped green cabbage (about 2 heads of cabbage)
2 cups zucchini, chopped
1 cup yellow summer squash, chopped
1 cup sweet onion, diced
1 ½ cup red bell pepper, chopped
1 ½ cup yellow bell pepper, chopped
¼ cup kosher salt
2 cups apple cider vinegar
1 ½ cup rice wine vinegar
1 ¼ cup sugar
1 ½ tablespoons mustard seeds
2 teaspoons celery seeds
2 teaspoons dry mustard
½ teaspoon ground ginger
½ teaspoon turmeric
4 hot dogs
4 buns

At Home: Combine the cabbage, zucchini, squash, sweet onion, red bell pepper and yellow bell pepper in a bowl and toss with the salt. Place the mixture in a colander in the sink and let it sweat for 3 hours.

Combine both vinegars, sugar, mustard seeds, celery seeds, dry mustard, ground ginger and turmeric in a large pot and bring to a boil.

Slowly add the vegetables and cook 10 minutes or until the cabbage begins to wilt. Once cooked, use a slotted spoon to divide the mixture between 7 sterilized canning jars (1-pint).

Divide the vinegar mixture evenly between the jars, filling until about ½ inch from the top. Wipe each jar clean, cover with metal lids, screw them tight to seal. Process each jar by boiling in water for 15 minutes. Remove from the water, cool completely, and check for proper seal by pressing a finger in the middle of the lid. If the lid springs up when you release your finger it has not sealed properly.

Store in a cool dark place for up to 1 year.

At Camp: Using green, sharpened sticks, cook your hot dogs over an open campfire, rotating slowly, for about 5 minutes or until fat is dripping into the fire and you have a good golden brown char on the outside of the hot dogs.

Serve in buns topped with chow chow.

SUGGESTED BEVERAGE: Cocktail - See 4th of July Cherry Crush.

Wine Marinated Steaks With Naan

⏲Serves 2→

My in-laws raise some of the best beef I have ever tasted on a farm just outside of Franktown, Colorado. It is grass-fed, which is leaner than standard beef, but when marinated this meat is delicious. You can find local grass-fed beef at many health food stores in Colorado. The longer you marinate these steaks the better, so I recommend starting at home before you drive up to the mountains.

½ lemon, thinly sliced

3 sprigs thyme

2 Fresno chiles, halved

9 garlic cloves, smashed

¾ cup dry red wine

¼ cup olive oil, plus splash to coat the grill

½ teaspoon freshly ground black pepper

¾ pound hanger steak, center membrane removed, cut into 2 pieces

4 tablespoons unsalted butter

1 shallot, sliced

himalayan salt and freshly ground black pepper to taste

1 package naan bread

At Home: In a large plastic baggie combine the lemon,

thyme, 1 chile, 6 garlic cloves, wine, olive oil and pepper. Make sure you smash the garlic cloves once so they release their flavor. Add the steaks and close the bag, turning to coat. Store in your cooler.

At Camp: Place a portable grill top over hot coals on your campfire or if you have access to a grill, prepare coals. Add butter to a small pan and melt. Chop 1 chile and remaining 3 garlic cloves and sauté with the shallot, in the butter until the shallots are soft, about 5 minutes. Season with salt and pepper and set aside near the fire to keep warm.

Remove the steak from the marinade and sprinkle with salt. Grill over direct heat for 6-7 minutes on each side for rare. Longer if you prefer medium or well done. Transfer the steak to a cutting board and let rest for 5 minutes.

While the steak rests, brush your naan bread with olive oil and grill on each side for 2 minutes, or until grill marks form and the bread is warmed through. Slice the steaks.

Evenly pour the shallot mixture over the steaks and serve with warm naan.

SUGGESTED BEVERAGE: American Tempranillo - Balistreri Vineyard (Denver, Colorado)

Vegetarian Paella

Serves 4 →

I have spent many summer nights dining outdoors on the beaches of Valencia on the Mediterranean coast of Spain. Paella originated in this region and there is no better dish suited for the outdoors. In fact, traditionally it is meant to be cooked over a big open flame. This vegetarian version leaves out the fresh seafood that can be hard to come by in Colorado and utilizes fresh local veggies instead.

2 large heirloom tomatoes, chopped
5 garlic cloves, minced
1 eggplant, cubed
¼ cup sweet peas
1 can artichokes, drained
1 tablespoon olive oil

2 cans cannellini beans, drained

1 pound short grain white rice

1 pinch saffron threads

4 cups vegetable broth

1 sprig fresh thyme

5 green olives

salt and freshly ground black pepper to taste
1 lemon, sliced

At Home: Combine the tomatoes, garlic, eggplant, peas and artichokes in a large plastic baggie and pack for camp.

At Camp: Heat a paella pan over hot coals on your campfire or on a portable gas stove and add the olive oil. When the oil is hot, add the vegetables you have stored in your plastic baggie and sauté for about 10 minutes.

Add the beans, stir well, then add the rice, spreading evenly in the pan. Stir slowly for a few minutes to make sure the ingredients are well mixed.

In a bowl or container combine the saffron and vegetable broth and mix. Pour the vegetable broth mixture slowly into the pan until the rice is covered completely. Add the thyme sprig to the middle of the paella.

Allow the paella to simmer, uncovered, for about 20 minutes, or until the rice is al dente. Do not stir during this time. We are trying to form a crunchy layer of rice on the bottom of the pan.

Remove from heat, add the olives and cover the pan, allowing the paella to sit for about 5 minutes. Sprinkle with salt and pepper and serve with lemon slices.

SUGGESTED BEVERAGE: Sangria - See Colorado Peach Sangria.

Jerk Chicken Campfire Kabobs

Serves 4

Kabobs are a natural fit for a campfire and many times I simply cook these on the end of a long, green stick, just as I would a hot dog or sausage. The blend of spices in this recipe makes for an extremely well seasoned and flavorful dish.

¼ cup dark brown sugar

¼ cup dark rum

3 tablespoons olive oil

2 tablespoons apple cider vinegar

1 habanero pepper, seeded and minced

6 green onions, chopped

6 garlic cloves

1 tablespoon fresh ginger, peeled and minced

2 teaspoons ground allspice

1 teaspoon pumpkin pie spice

3 boneless, skinless chicken breasts, cut into large cubes

½ fresh pineapple, peeled, cored and cubed

salt to taste

At Home: Prepare the rub by combining the sugar, rum, oil, vinegar, pepper, 3 green onions, garlic, ginger, allspice, and pumpkin pie spice in a food processor. Pulse until it becomes a smooth paste.

Transfer the rub into a large plastic bag or tupperware and add the cubed chicken, toss to coat, and store in a cold cooler to marinate as you drive to camp.

At Camp: Using either a fresh green stick or kabob skewers, thread the chicken, scallions and pineapple alternately on the skewers. Sprinkle salt on each.

Cook over hot coals in the campfire for 15 minutes, rotating every 5 minutes to cook evenly on all sides. Make sure the chicken is cooked through, until white in the middle.

Serve hot.

SUGGESTED BEVERAGE: Shrub - See Blood Orange Ginger Shrubs.

Rosemary Colorado Lamb Sloppy Joes

Serves 4

Colorado produces some pretty amazing lamb from some amazing farms around the state. Make sure you buy high quality lamb to get the most from this recipe. These dinner sandwiches are messy, saucy and full of flavor.

1 lb ground lamb

1 yellow onion, finely chopped

3 garlic cloves, minced

1 15 oz can tomato puree

¼ cup honey

2 teaspoons fresh rosemary leaves, chopped

salt and freshly ground black pepper to taste

2 tablespoons goat cheese

4 hamburger buns

Heat a large cast iron skillet over a campfire or portable gas stove for 3 minutes. Add the ground lamb and brown, cooking for about 10 minutes, stirring often and breaking up large chunks with a spoon.

Remove the meat from the skillet, reserving about 1 tablespoon of the fat in the pan. Pour the rest of the fat into the fire to discard and return the meat to the pan.

Add the onion and garlic and cook about 5 minutes or until the onion begins to brown. Add the tomato puree, honey and rosemary and cook for 4 minutes. Remove from heat and add salt and pepper.

Divide and spread the goat cheese evenly on the top half of each of the 4 buns. Spoon lamb mixture evenly on the bottom half of the buns, top with the goat cheese half and serve hot.

SUGGESTED BEVERAGE: Dale's Pale Ale - Oskar Blues Brewery (Lyons, Colorado)

Vegetarian Campfire Nachos

Serves 4

The ultimate sharing dish, nachos are a favorite camping meal of mine. Cooking them in a skillet over a campfire gives them a smokey flavor that is not replicable in your home kitchen.

1 14.5 oz can black beans, drained

¼ cup red onion, chopped

2 teaspoons ground cumin

2 teaspoons chile powder

salt to taste

1 bag corn tortilla chips

1 8 oz jar salsa

1 cup frozen sweet corn, thawed

2 cups sharp cheddar cheese, grated

1 6 oz can black olives, drained

1 avocado, diced

1 4 oz can pickled jalapeños, drained

Heat a large cast iron skillet over a campfire or portable gas stove for 3 minutes. While the skillet heats, combine the black beans, red onion, cumin, chile powder and salt in a large bowl, stirring well to mix.

Place half the chips in the skillet and top with the black

bean mixture. Top with half the salsa, sweet corn and half the cheese.

Layer the other half of the chips on top of the cheese, topping with the remaining cheese, followed by the olives.

Cover the skillet with tinfoil, allowing a few holes for moisture to escape and cook over hot coals for 10 minutes, or until the cheese has melted and you can hear the sizzling of beans and chips.

Remove from heat, top with avocado and pickled jalapeños. Serve warm with remaining salsa on the side.

SUGGESTED BEVERAGE: Margarita - See Snowflake Berry Margarita.

Foraged Porcini Mushroom Sausage Dinner

Serves 4

There is nothing like earthy foraged porcini mushrooms and they shine in this easy foil dinner. If you can't find them or don't have the time to look, substitute with your favorite store bought mushrooms.

1 teaspoon onion powder

1 teaspoon garlic powder

1 teaspoon pink himalayan salt

1 teaspoon dried parsley

1 teaspoon turmeric

1 teaspoon freshly ground black pepper

3 large bratwurst links

2 lbs small red potatoes, cut in half

1 lb multicolored carrots, cut into 1 inch pieces

1 sweet yellow onion, sliced

2 foraged porcini mushrooms, sliced

¼ cup unsalted butter, cubed

2 tablespoons soy sauce

At Home: In a small plastic baggie mix the onion powder, garlic powder, salt, parsley, turmeric and pepper. Store and pack for camp.

At Camp: On a flat surface lay out 4 large sheets of tinfoil. Cut the bratwurst into thirds, divide them evenly with the potatoes, carrots, onion and mushrooms, between the 4 sheets of foil. Dot each pile with butter and evenly sprinkle the pre-made spice mix over the top. Add equal parts soy sauce to each foil packet.

Bring the edges of the foil together, crimp the edges to seal tightly and place each packet on hot coals in the campfire.

Cook for 25 – 30 minutes, rotating twice, or until the sausage is no longer pink and the vegetables are tender.

Remove from the fire, open the packets, and serve hot.

SUGGESTED BEVERAGE: Iced Tea - See Wild Mint Sun Tea.

FORAGING TIPS: The rule with mushroom foraging is, if you don't know what it is or are not sure, don't eat it, so make sure you take care when selecting mushrooms. Porcini mushrooms, which are my personal favorite, can be found June through August in Colorado. Porcini mushrooms are normally a brown or reddish brown color and found at higher elevations, typically around 10,000 feet. The stem is thick and the cap can sometimes be sticky.

Chilaquiles With Salsa Verde

⏲Serves 4 →

Chilaquiles are a favorite of mine from Mexico. I usually prepare this dish in a large cast iron skillet at home but I like the smoke flavor that comes from cooking over open flames.

11 tomatillos

2 garlic cloves

½ red onion, chopped
¼ jalapeño, with seeds

1 teaspoon sugar

½ teaspoon salt

1 cup fresh cilantro, chopped
1 tablespoon olive oil

2 poblano chiles

1 cooked chicken breast, shredded

2 cups low-sodium chicken broth

freshly ground black pepper to taste

1 bag white corn tortilla chips

¼ cup sour cream

2 tablespoons queso fresco, crumbled

At Home: Husk the outer papery layer from the tomatillos, rinse and quarter each. Place the tomatillos in a medium sauce pan and cover them with water. Bing to a boil and cook, uncovered, for about 7 minutes. Drain.

In a blender or food processor, combine the garlic, ¼ cup of the red onion, jalapeño, sugar and ¼ teaspoon salt and puree until smooth. Add half of the cilantro and the tomatillos and puree again until smooth. Store the salsa in a ball jar or tupperware and pack in a cooler for camp.

At Camp: Over hot coals in a campfire or over a portable gas stove, heat the olive oil in a large cast iron skillet.

While the skillet heats up, stick your poblano chiles on a green stick and roast them over the campfire. Alternatively you could place them on a portable grill top over hot coals. Roast them for about 10 minutes, turning multiple times, until the outer skin is bubbly and charred. Remove from heat and place in a bowl, cover with a lid and allow them to sit.

Add chicken to the skillet and cook for a few minutes, then add the salsa, stirring, allowing it to simmer and thicken for about 5 minutes. Remove chiles from the bowl, peel the outer skin and seed. Chop into thin strips and add to the skillet along with the broth, pepper and ¼ teaspoon salt.

Simmer, uncovered for 10 minutes, then add 4 handfuls of the tortilla chips to the sauce. Heat for 2 minutes. Serve hot with sour cream, queso fresco and extra chips.

SUGGESTED BEVERAGE: Margarita - See Snowflake Berry Margarita.

Honey Chicken And Biscuit Sandwiches

⚐Serves 4→

This could easily be a breakfast meal as well, but if you are the type that likes breakfast for dinner, then this sandwich will blow your mind. It is the perfect combination of salt and sweet. I usually buy store bought biscuits for this recipe, as I would a loaf of bread, but you can always make them fresh if you prefer.

¼ cup buttermilk
2 tablespoons garlic hot sauce
3 boneless skinless chicken breasts
2 cups olive oil
2 cups all purpose flour
½ teaspoon salt
1 teaspoon freshly ground black pepper
4 store bought biscuits
2 tablespoons Colorado honey
½ cup sliced dill pickles
2 tablespoons stone ground mustard

At Home: Whisk together the buttermilk and hot sauce. Cut each chicken breast in half and add to a large plastic baggie along with the buttermilk marinade. Shake to coat. Pack in an ice filled cooler for camp.

At Camp: Add the oil to a large cast iron skillet and heat over hot coals or a portable gas stove. In a bowl mix the flour, salt and pepper.

Remove the chicken from the bag and dredge in the flour mixture, coating each piece of chicken completely. Carefully place the chicken pieces into the hot oil and fry, turning over several times, for 25 minutes, or until the chicken is cooked through.

Remove the chicken, piece by piece, allowing it to drip for a minute before setting it on a paper towel lined plate.

Cut each biscuit in half and evenly layer on pieces of hot chicken, drizzled honey, pickles and mustard. Top with the other biscuit half and serve immediately.

SUGGESTED BEVERAGE: Shift Pale Lager – New Belgium Brewing (Ft. Collins, Colorado)

Colorado Beer Brats

⟶Serves 6⟶

Beer brats are a summer classic and thanks to Colorado craft beer, this recipe becomes a local star.

4 cans of your favorite Colorado craft beer
1 large yellow onion, sliced
6 bratwurst
2 teaspoons red pepper flakes
1 teaspoon garlic powder
1 ½ teaspoon pink himalayan salt
1 teaspoon freshly ground black pepper
6 hot dog buns
stone ground mustard

Fill a disposable aluminum foil cooking pan with beer. I like using a 9" square aluminum cake pan.

Add the onions to the beer and place over hot coals over the campfire. Bring to a slow simmer and add the bratwurst, red pepper flakes, garlic powder, salt and pepper. Cook for about 10 minutes and remove the brats. Leave the onions to continue cooking.

Finish cooking the brats on green camping sticks, or on a portable grill rack roasting them over the fire, rotating slowly for about 5 minutes.

Serve in hot dog buns, topped with the the cooked onion mixture and mustard.

SUGGESTED BEVERAGE: Craft Lager – Upslope Brewing Company (Boulder, Colorado)

Elk Meatballs

Serves 6 →

I spent several years in Spain and grew to love their albondigas, or meatballs. I have adapted the traditional Spanish recipe for garlic tomato sauce albondigas and given it a Colorado twist.

1 pound ground elk
1 small yellow onion, chopped
1 tablespoon parsley flakes
2 tablespoons milk
1 teaspoon salt
1 tablespoon Worcestershire sauce
¼ teaspoon nutmeg
¼ teaspoon thyme
½ cup bread crumbs
¼ cup olive oil, plus 1 tablespoon
4 garlic cloves, minced
1 33 oz can whole tomatoes
1 teaspoon dried oregano
salt and freshly ground black pepper to taste
fresh loaf of bakery bread

At Home: In a large bowl combine the elk, onion, parsley, milk, salt, Worcestershire sauce, nutmeg, thyme and bread crumbs. Using your hands, mold bite sized portions of elk into meatballs. Store in tupperware in a cold cooler for camp.

At Camp: Heat ¼ cup of the olive oil in a large dutch oven over hot coals or a portable gas stove. Add the elk meatballs and brown on all sides in the oil, about 5 minutes.

Remove the meatballs from the oil and put them in a bowl or on a plate.

Add the additional tablespoon of olive oil to the skillet, followed by the garlic, tomatoes with juice, and oregano. Break up the tomatoes with a spoon, add the meatballs and simmer, covered for about 30 minutes. Stir occasionally.

Remove from heat, season with salt and pepper and serve with thick slices of fresh bread.

SUGGESTED BEVERAGE: Sangria - See Colorado Peach Sangria.

Mustard Butternut Squash And Kale

Serves 4

This dish can be served as a light dinner or even as a heavy side. I enjoy it on longer camping trips when I grow tired of meat heavy dishes. For mustard lovers, this is a must try dinner.

3 tablespoons olive oil
1 lb butternut squash, cut into small cubes
1 bunch kale, torn
1 cup low-sodium chicken broth
1 tablespoon whole grain mustard
Salt and freshly ground black pepper to taste

Heat the olive oil in a large dutch oven over a campfire. Add the butternut squash, and cook, stirring occasionally, for 10 minutes, or until the squash begins to soften.

Add the kale, chicken broth, mustard, salt and pepper. Cook, stirring occasionally, for 10 minutes, or until tender.

Serve warm.

SUGGESTED BEVERAGE: Peacemaker Pilsner — Pug Ryan's Brewing Company (Dillon, Colorado)

Smoked Fingerling Potato Skillet Supper

Serves 4 →

I threw this dish together on a busy weeknight, utilizing what I had on hand in the garden and kitchen. An experiment gone right, this is now a common dinner I enjoy camping. I love smoked paprika, which adds depth to this dish, especially when cooked over a campfire.

¼ cup olive oil

1 lb fingerling potatoes

freshly ground black pepper and salt to taste

1 tablespoon smoked paprika

4 garlic cloves, minced

1 bunch kale, torn

4 eggs

Heat a large cast iron skillet over a campfire and add the olive oil, letting it heat for a few minutes.

Add the fingerling potatoes and some salt. Cover and cook for 15 minutes, stirring several times. Add the smoked paprika and garlic, stir and cook for 5 minutes longer, or until the garlic becomes fragrant.

Add the kale to the top of the potatoes and cover again, cooking for an additional 3 minutes, or until the greens begin to wilt.

Using a spatula or spoon, make 4 small circular spaces in the pan. You want the eggs to have direct contact with the bottom of the skillet while also staying relatively contained in a small potato circle.

Crack the eggs adding them 1 by 1 to each space in the pan. Sprinkle a pinch of smoked paprika and pepper on each egg and cover again, cooking for 4 minutes or until the eggs are just medium done. You want the yolks to remain runny.

Remove from heat and serve the eggs on a bed of potatoes and greens.

SUGGESTED BEVERAGE: Cocktail - See Foraged Spruce Tip Gin Cocktails.

Grilled Pesto And Pepper Sandwiches

Serves 4

These vegetarian sandwiches are a vegetable lovers dream. Smokey fire grilled vegetables pair perfectly with pesto and mozzarella cheese.

1 red bell pepper, sliced
1 zucchini, sliced lengthwise
1 red onion, thickly sliced
1 yellow squash, sliced lengthwise
4 tablespoons olive oil
salt and freshly ground black pepper to taste
1 loaf ciabatta bread, sliced in half lengthwise
¾ cup basil pesto
1 ball fresh mozzarella, thickly sliced

In a bowl combine the bell pepper, zucchini, red onion, and squash with the olive oil. Tossing to coat well. Add salt and pepper to coat.

Brush some additional olive oil on the cut sides of the bread. On a portable grill rack, grill the vegetables over hot coals for 5 minutes, per side. Grill the bread for 2 minutes on each side, or until toasted.

Remove everything from the grill rack and spread a good amount of pesto on the bottom half (cut side) of the bread.

Separate the onion and layer rings on the pesto. Follow this with a layer of mozzarella, then grilled vegetables. Top with the remaining half of the ciabatta loaf and cut the sandwich into 4 large sandwich wedges before serving.

SUGGESTED BEVERAGE: Back Ally White Can – The Infinite Monkey Theorem (Denver, Colorado)

Purple Potato Pizza

⏺Serves 4→

This pizza is as colorful as it is delicious and cooked over flames outside, it is positively delightful. If you can't find purple sweet potatoes, regular sweet potatoes are a great swap.

½ cup olive oil
1 purple sweet potato, thinly sliced
1 russet potato, thinly sliced
salt and freshly ground black pepper to taste
store bought pizza dough
½ cup crumbled feta cheese
6 kalamata olives, sliced
1 sprig fresh rosemary, leaves removed from the stick

In large cast Iron skillet, heat the olive oil, then add the potatoes, browning them, for about 10 minutes. Flip them to cook on the opposite side and cook for another 10 minutes.

Sprinkle salt and pepper over the top of the potatoes and remove the skillet from heat.

Roll out the pizza dough on a flat surface and gently lay it on a portable grill rack over hot coals in your fire. Cook for about 3 minutes on each side, until lightly crisped.

Remove the dough from heat and spoon some of the olive oil left in the skillet, about 2 tablespoons, evenly over the top of the crust. Spread it evenly, as you would pizza sauce, over the surface.

Evenly add the cooked potato slices as the first layer on the top of the pizza. Follow with a layer of feta cheese, kalamata olives and rosemary. Return the pizza back to the grill rack.

Cook over hot coals for about 8 minutes. Remove from heat, slice and serve.

SUGGESTED BEVERAGE: Noche – Alfred Eames Cellars (Paonia, Colorado)

Foil Sweet Potatoes With Black Bean Salsa

Serves 2

Baked sweet potatoes offer complex flavors that also happen to be good for you. I also like sweet potatoes because they tend to cook slightly quicker, which can be nice when cooking in a fire. This hearty vegetarian dish satisfies even the hungriest of campers.

2 large sweet potatoes

salt and freshly ground black pepper to taste

1 15 oz can black beans, drained

1 small tomato, diced

1 jalapeño, seeded and minced

2 tablespoons fresh cilantro, chopped

¼ cup red onion, chopped

1 tablespoon olive oil

2 limes, juiced

¾ cup extra sharp raw cheddar cheese, shredded

Sprinkle the potatoes with salt and pepper and enclose completely in large sheets of tinfoil. Place the packages on hot coals in the fire and cook for 45 minutes to an hour, rotating at least once.

While the potatoes cook, mix the beans, tomato, jalapeño, cilantro, onion, olive oil, lime juice, salt and pepper together in a large bowl.

When the potatoes are done, remove them from the fire and allow to cool for a few minutes, until cool enough to handle.

Cut the potatoes in half lengthwise and shred the potatoes with a fork. Add half the cheese to each hot potato, then spoon half of the black bean salsa evenly over each potato.

Serve immediately.

SUGGESTED BEVERAGE: Cocktail - See Snowflake Berry Margarita.

www.ingramcontent.com/pod-product-compliance
Lightning Source LLC
Chambersburg PA
CBHW071439070526
44578CB00001B/145